영어 리딩 학습의 최종 목표는 논픽션 독해력 향상에 있습니다.

학년이 올라갈수록 영어 시험 출제의 비중이 높아지는 논픽션. 우리는 논픽션 리딩을 통해 다양한 분야의 어휘와 지식을 습득하고 문제 해결 능력을 키울 수 있습니다. 또한 생활 속 실용문과 시험 상황의 복잡한 지문을 이해하고 분석하며, 나에게 필요한 정보를 추출하는 연습을 할 수 있습니다. 논픽션 독해력은 비판적 사고와 논리적 사고를 발전시키고, 영어로 표현된 아이디어를 깊이 있게 이해하고 효과적으로 소통하는 언어 능력을 갖출 수 있도록 도와줍니다.

미국교과서는 논픽션 리딩에 가장 적합한 학습 도구입니다.

미국교과서는 과학, 사회과학, 역사, 예술, 문학 등 다양한 주제의 폭넓은 지식과 이해를 제공하며, 사실을 그대로 받아들이는 능력뿐만 아니라 텍스트 너머의 맥락에 대한 비판적 사고와 분석 능력도 함께 배울 수 있도록 구성되어 있습니다. 미국 교과과정 주제의 리딩을 통해 학생들은 현실적인 주제를 탐구하고, 아카데믹한 어휘를 학습하면서 논리적 탐구의 방법을 함께 배울 수 있습니다. 미국교과서는 논픽션 독해력 향상을 위한 최고의 텍스트입니다.

탁월한 논픽션 독해력을 원한다면
미국교과서 READING 시리즈

(1) 미국교과서의 핵심 주제들을 엄선하여 담은 지문을 읽으며 **독해력**이 향상되고 **배경지식**이 쌓입니다.

(2) 가지고 있는 지식과 새로운 정보를 연결해 내 것으로 만드는 **통합사고력**을 기를 수 있습니다.

(3) 꼼꼼히 읽고 완전히 소화할 수 있도록 하는 수준별 독해 훈련으로 **문제 해결력**이 향상됩니다.

(4) 기초 문장 독해에서 추론까지, 학습자의 **수준별로 선택하여 학습**할 수 있도록 난이도를 설계하였습니다.

(5) 스스로 계획하고 점검하며 실력을 쌓아가는 **자기주도력**이 형성됩니다.

Author Suejeong Shin

She has been an adjunct professor of English Education at Yonsei University since 2017. Her research centers around the implementation of cognitive psychology to foster literacy development among young English language learners in Korea. In addition to her role in the classroom, she demonstrates visionary leadership as the founder of We Read, a literacy company.

With an impressive collection of sixty children's picture book titles and over 200 literacy-focused textbooks, she is an accomplished author and an expert in her field. She actively engages in the development of an innovative literacy curation service, ensuring that children have positive reading experiences in English. Equipped with a Ph.D. in cognitive science from Yonsei University, Suejeong's transformative work can be further explored on her captivating website at www.drsue.co.kr.

미국교과서 **READING LEVEL 2 ❸**
American Textbook Reading *Second Edition*

Second Published on August 14, 2023
Second Printed on August 30, 2023

First Published on November 27, 2015

Written by Suejeong Shin
Researcher Dain Song
Editorial Manager Namhui Kim, Seulgi Han
Design Kichun Jang, Hyeonsook Lee
Development Editor Mina Park
Proofreading Ryan P. Lagace, Benjamin Schultz
Typesetting Yeon Design
Illustrations Eunhyung Ryu, Hyoju Kim, Jongeun Yang
Recording Studio YR Media
Photo Credit shutterstock.com

Published and distributed by Gilbutschool

56, Worldcup-ro 10-gil, Mapo-gu, Seoul, Korea, 121-842
Tel 02-332-0931
Fax 02-322-0586
Homepage www.gilbutschool.co.kr
Publisher Jongwon Lee

ISBN   979-11-6406-543-1 (64740)
          979-11-6406-536-3 (set)
(Gilbutschool code : 30541)

READING

미국교과서 리딩

LEVEL 2 ③

길벗스쿨

LEVEL 2 논픽션 리딩 시작

1

미국 교과과정 주제의 픽션(50%)과 논픽션(50%) 지문을 고루 읽으며 균형 있는 읽기 실력을 키웁니다.

학생들의 인지 수준과 흥미를 반영한 다양한 토픽으로 하나의 주제 아래 Fiction과 Nonfiction 지문을 고루 읽을 수 있습니다. 이와 같은 반복적인 접근을 통하여 교과 주제에 더욱 익숙해지고 생각의 폭을 넓힐 수 있습니다.

2

기초 논픽션 주제 어휘와 패턴 문형을 중심으로 다양한 형식의 글을 학습합니다.

본격 논픽션 리딩 학습을 시작하기 전, 반복되는 패턴 문형 안에서 낯선 논픽션 어휘에 적응할 수 있도록 합니다. 또한 스토리 형식이나 설명문과 더불어 메뉴판, 편지글, 안내문 등 다양한 문형을 통하여 실용적인 텍스트를 이해하는 기초를 다집니다.

3

간단한 문장 구조의 글을 읽고, 다양한 문제를 경험하며 독해의 기본기를 튼튼하게 합니다.

지문을 읽고 핵심 주제, 세부 내용, 감정 표현, 문장 완성하기 등 다양한 문제를 통하여 읽은 내용을 파악합니다. 선택지에서 지문과 일치하는 부분을 찾아 단순히 답을 고르기 보다는 한번 더 생각하고 문제를 해결할 수 있도록 구성하여 독해의 기본기를 다집니다.

4

도표를 활용한 전체 내용 통합 활동으로 기초 리딩 스킬을 연습합니다.

도표 활동은 글의 구조를 확인하는 것과 동시에 어휘를 활용하는 능력에도 큰 도움이 됩니다. 길지 않은 지문이지만, 세부적인 내용을 확인한 이후 전체적으로 내용을 통합하고 정리하는 활동을 통하여 리딩 스킬을 익힐 수 있습니다.

자기주도 학습 계획표

Week 1

UNIT 01	UNIT 02	UNIT 03	UNIT 04
Student Book ☐	Student Book ☐	Student Book ☐	Student Book ☐
Workbook ☐	Workbook ☐	Workbook ☐	Workbook ☐

DATE

Week 2

UNIT 05	UNIT 06	UNIT 07	UNIT 08
Student Book ☐	Student Book ☐	Student Book ☐	Student Book ☐
Workbook ☐	Workbook ☐	Workbook ☐	Workbook ☐

DATE

Week 3

UNIT 09	UNIT 10	UNIT 11	UNIT 12
Student Book ☐	Student Book ☐	Student Book ☐	Student Book ☐
Workbook ☐	Workbook ☐	Workbook ☐	Workbook ☐

DATE

Week 4

UNIT 13	UNIT 14	UNIT 15	UNIT 16
Student Book ☐	Student Book ☐	Student Book ☐	Student Book ☐
Workbook ☐	Workbook ☐	Workbook ☐	Workbook ☐

DATE

Week 5

UNIT 17	UNIT 18	UNIT 19	UNIT 20
Student Book ☐	Student Book ☐	Student Book ☐	Student Book ☐
Workbook ☐	Workbook ☐	Workbook ☐	Workbook ☐

DATE

★ 이 책의 구성과 학습법 ★

Before Reading

배경지식을 묻는 질문에 답하고,
주제별 어휘를 익히며 글의 내용을 예측해 봅니다.

QR코드를 스캔하여
정확한 발음 확인하기

Talk About It

경험을 묻는 질문에 답하며
주제를 대략적으로 파악해
보고, 배경지식을 활성화
합니다.

Words to Know

단어를 듣고 따라 말하며
익히고, 그림을 통해 뜻을
유추합니다.

Reading

미국교과서 핵심 주제의 픽션, 논픽션 글을 읽으며
교과 지식과 독해력을 쌓습니다.

Reading Passage

제목과 그림을 통해 내용을
먼저 예측해 봅니다.
음원을 들으면서 글을 읽고,
중심 내용과 세부 내용을
파악합니다.

Key Expressions

글에 사용된 패턴 문형
대화를 듣고 따라 말하며
익힙니다.

After Reading

다양한 유형의 문제를 풀며 읽은 내용을 확인하고,
단어와 문장을 점검합니다.

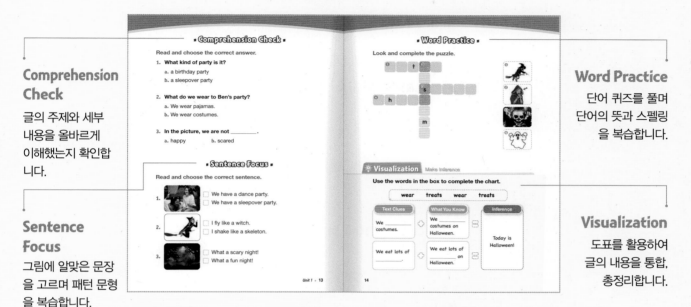

Comprehension Check

글의 주제와 세부 내용을 올바르게 이해했는지 확인합니다.

Sentence Focus

그림에 알맞은 문장을 고르며 패턴 문형을 복습합니다.

Word Practice

단어 퀴즈를 풀며 단어의 뜻과 스펠링을 복습합니다.

Visualization

도표를 활용하여 글의 내용을 통합, 총정리합니다.

Workbook

핵심 어휘와 주요 문장을 복습합니다.

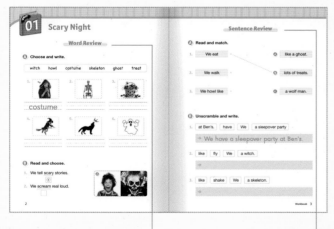

Word Review

이미지를 활용하여 단어의 의미를 복습합니다.

Sentence Review

문장 완성하기, 순서 배열하기 활동으로 패턴 문형과 어순을 복습합니다.

무료 온라인 학습 자료

길벗스쿨 e클래스

(eclass.gilbut.co.kr)에 접속하시면 〈미국교과서 READING〉 시리즈에 대한 상세 정보 및 부가학습 자료를 무료로 이용하실 수 있습니다.

1. 음원 스트리밍 및 MP3 파일
2. 추가 워크시트 4종
   단어 테스트, 문장 따라 쓰기, 해석 테스트, 리딩 지문 테스트
3. 복습용 온라인 퀴즈

★ 목차 ★

Scary Night

Talk About It

1 Have you ever slept over at a friend's house?
2 What did you do there?

· Words to Know ·

Listen and repeat.

costume

scream

scary

treat

ghost

witch

howl

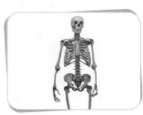

skeleton

Scary Night

We have a sleepover
party at Ben's.

We wear costumes and
scream real loud.
We tell scary stories and eat lots of treats.
We play lots of games and dance to the beat.
We walk like a ghost.
We fly like a witch.
We howl like a wolf man.
We shake like a skeleton.

Oh, what a scary night!

Key Expressions
A : What did you do at Ben's party?
B : I walked like a ghost.

12

Comprehension Check

Read and choose the correct answer.

1. **What kind of party is it?**

   a. a birthday party

   b. a sleepover party

2. **What do we wear to Ben's party?**

   a. We wear pajamas.

   b. We wear costumes.

3. **In the picture, we are not _____ .**

   a. happy   **b.** scared

Sentence Focus

Read and choose the correct sentence.

1.
   ☐ We have a dance party.
   ☐ We have a sleepover party.

2.
   ☐ I fly like a witch.
   ☐ I shake like a skeleton.

3.
   ☐ What a scary night!
   ☐ What a fun night!

■ Word Practice ■

Look and complete the puzzle.

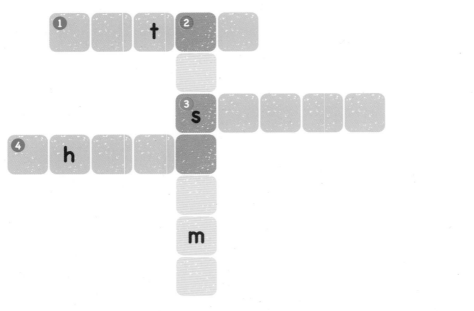

☀ Visualization Make Inference

Use the words in the box to complete the chart.

wear   treats   wear   treats

Text Clues		What You Know		Inference
We _____ costumes.	➕	We _____ costumes on Halloween.	＝	
We eat lots of _____ .	➕	We eat lots of _____ on Halloween.	＝	Today is Halloween!

The Laser Maze

Talk About It 🎧

1 What games do you know?
2 Do you know any games to play late at night?

Words to Know

Listen and repeat. 🎧

laser

maze

hallway

crepe paper

navigate

adjust

stopwatch

player

The Laser Maze

Make a Laser Maze

Make a laser maze in the hallway.
Cut strips of crepe paper.
Tape one end high. Tape the other end low.
Tape strips all along the hallway.
Try to navigate through the laser maze.
Adjust the laser maze.

How to Play

The round begins with starting the stopwatch.
Each player navigates through the laser maze.
The players may not touch the maze strips.
Time the race.
The fastest player wins the game.

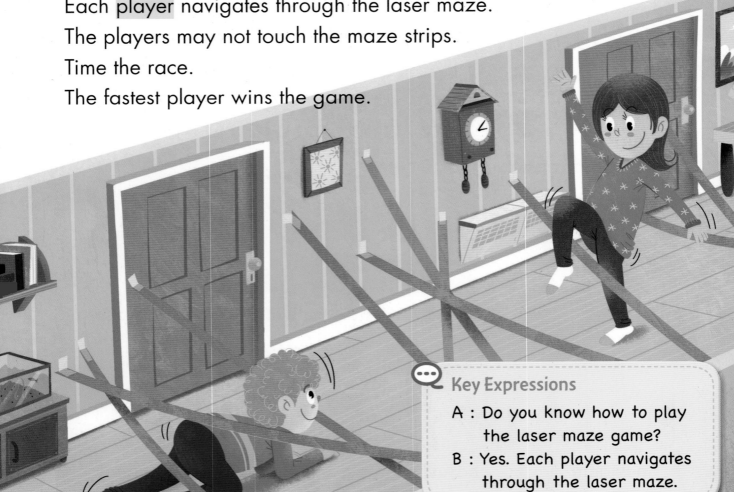

💬 **Key Expressions**

A : Do you know how to play the laser maze game?
B : Yes. Each player navigates through the laser maze.

Comprehension Check

Read and choose the correct answer.

1. **What is the reading about?**

   a. It's about a laser maze.

   b. It's about a fun night.

2. **What do you need to make a laser maze?**

   a. a laser

   b. crepe paper and tape

3. **It's fun to _____ through the laser maze.**

   a. navigate   **b.** touch

Sentence Focus

Read and choose the correct sentence.

1.  ☐ Tape the crepe paper high.
   ☐ Tape the crepe paper low.

2.  ☐ The round begins with touching the maze.
   ☐ The round begins with starting the stopwatch.

3. ☐ The fastest player wins the game.
   ☐ The fastest player begins the race.

▪ Word Practice ▪

Look and complete the puzzle.

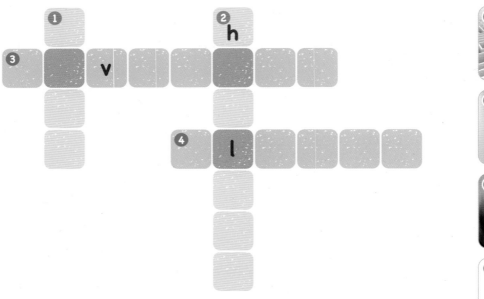

⚙ Visualization   Main Idea & Details

Use the words in the box to complete the chart.

> Adjust   stopwatch

The Laser Maze

How to Make
- Make it in the hallway.
- Cut and tape strips of crepe paper.
- _____ the laser maze.

How to Play
- Start the _____.
- Navigate through the laser maze.
- Time the race.
- The fastest player wins.

My Best Birthday

Talk About It 🎧

1 What do you like to do with your dad?

2 Have you ever been to a baseball game?

▪ Words to Know ▪

Listen and repeat. 🎧

baseball

enter

score

tie

home plate

pitch

strike

swing

My Best Birthday 🎧

It was my birthday.
Dad took me out to a baseball game.

The Bears entered the stadium.
"Go, Bears, go!" we cheered for the home team.

At the second half of the last inning,
the score was a tie.
The batter for the Bears stood at
home plate and waited.
The first pitch was a fastball.
"Strike one!"
The next pitch was slow.
The batter swung hard and
C-R-A-C-K!
POW!
Up, up went the ball!

It was my best birthday ever!

Key Expressions

A : What did you do on your birthday?
B : Dad took me out to a baseball game.

Comprehension Check

Read and choose the correct answer.

1. **Where did I go on my birthday?**

    a. I went to a baseball game.

    b. I went to a basketball game.

2. **What made my birthday the best birthday?**

    a. the Bears' win

    b. playing baseball

3. **The Bears is the _____ team.**

    a. home   b. second

Sentence Focus

Read and choose the correct sentence.

1.
    ☐ The players entered the stadium.
    ☐ The players cheered in the stadium.

2.
    ☐ The score was a tie.
    ☐ The score was 3 to 2.

3.
    ☐ Mom took me out to a baseball game.
    ☐ I watched a baseball game on TV.

▪ Word Practice ▪

Look and complete the puzzle.

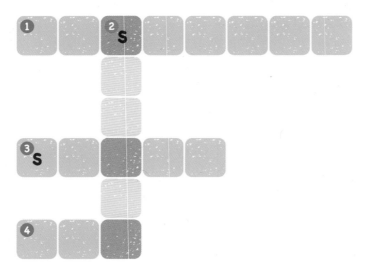

Visualization Setting

Use the words in the box to complete the chart.

baseball   tie

Where?

at the _____ game

What?

· We cheered for the home team.
· The score was a _____.
· The batter swung hard and crack!
· It was my best birthday ever!

We Love and Care

Talk About It 🎧

1 How many people are in your family?
2 What do you like to do with your family?

▪ Words to Know ▪

Listen and repeat. 🎧

mother

father

member

feed

guitar

family

have fun

hide-and-seek

We Love and Care 🎧

Families can be very different.
Some children live with only one parent.
Other children live with their mothers and fathers.

Family members help each other.
Nate helps his father by feeding the dog.
Amy's mother teaches Amy to play the guitar.

Family members have fun together.
John bakes a cake with his father.
Vera plays hide-and-seek with
her mother.

Family members love each other.

💬 Key Expressions
A : How do you help your
    parents?
B : I help my father by
    feeding the dog.

Comprehension Check

Read and choose the correct answer.

1. What is the reading about?

a. It's about families.

b. It's about children.

2. How are some families different?

a. Some children have fun with their parents.

b. Some children live with only one parent.

3. Families can be different, but they all _____ each other.

a. live   b. love

Sentence Focus

Read and choose the correct sentence.

1.
☐ Family members help each other.
☐ Family members can be different.

2.
☐ Her mother teaches her to play the guitar.
☐ Her mother teaches her to bake a cake.

3.
☐ He helps his father by feeding the dog.
☐ He helps his father by playing the guitar.

Word Practice

Look and complete the puzzle.

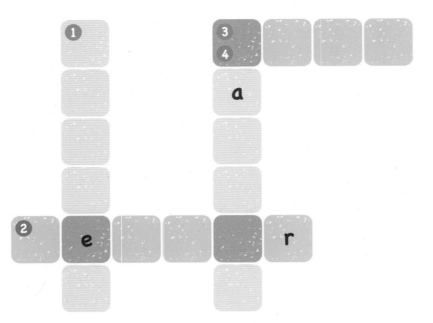

Visualization Compare & Contrast

Use the words in the box to complete the chart.

fun   help

Some Families
- live with only one parent

Family members
- _____ each other
- have _____ together
- love each other

Other Families
- live with their mothers and fathers

The Treehouse

Talk About It 🎧

1 Do you have a dream home?
2 What would you like to share about your dream home?

• Words to Know •

Listen and repeat. 🎧

build

treehouse

wood

nail

trunk

climb

board

order

The Treehouse

I'm going to build a treehouse
in the backyard.
I can do lots of cool things in it.
I start to build the treehouse
with a little help from Grandpa.

We cut some wood.
We nail the wood to the trunk for climbing up.
We nail the wood for the floor.
We nail the wood for the walls.
We put up the board for the roof.

"What do you want to do now?"
asks Grandpa.
"Let's order some pizza!" I cry.
It's cool to eat pizza in my treehouse.

Key Expressions

A : What do you want to do now?
B : Let's order some pizza!

28

▪ Comprehension Check ▪

Read and choose the correct answer.

1. **What am I doing?**

   a. I am building a treehouse.

   b. I am helping Grandpa.

2. **What do I want to do in my treehouse?**

   a. I want to eat pizza in my treehouse.

   b. I want to order a treehouse.

3. **My _____ is in the backyard.**

   a. treehouse   **b.** bicycle

▪ Sentence Focus ▪

Read and choose the correct sentence.

1.
   ☐ I cut the wood.
   ☐ I nail the wood.

2.
   ☐ I put up the board for the roof.
   ☐ I nail the board for the walls.

3.
   ☐ Grandpa helps me to climb up my treehouse.
   ☐ Grandpa helps me to build a treehouse.

▪ Word Practice ▪

Look and complete the puzzle.

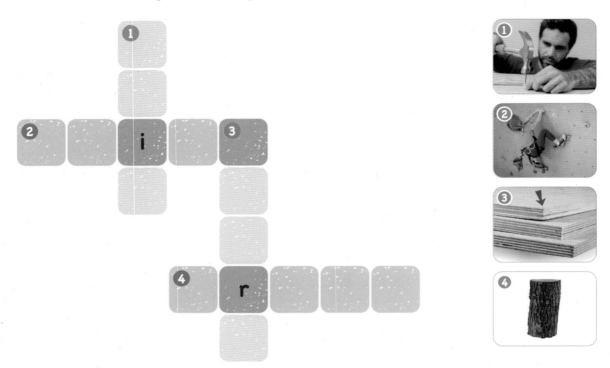

Visualization Setting

Use the words in the box to complete the chart.

build   order

Where?		What?
In my backyard	⌒	Grandpa and I _____ a treehouse.
In my treehouse	⌒	Grandpa and I _____ some pizza.

Pizza for Kings and Queens

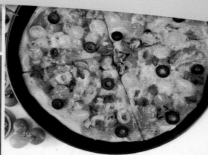

Talk About It

1 Do you like pizza?
2 What's your favorite pizza?

Words to Know

Listen and repeat.

Italy

king

visit

pizzeria

baker

Italian flag

basil

everyone

Pizza for Kings and Queens 🎧

Margherita pizza came from Italy.
It was named after Queen Margherita.

King Umberto I and Queen Margherita
visited Naples in 1889.
The king and queen went to a pizzeria.
They asked for a special pizza.
The baker made a pizza of the Italian flag.
He used basil for green.
He used cheese for white.
He used tomatoes for red.
The king and queen loved it.

These days, Margherita pizza is
not only for kings and queens.
It's for everyone.

▲ Queen Margherita

💬 **Key Expressions**

A : Where did Margherita
pizza come from?
B : It came from Italy.

▪ Comprehension Check ▪

Read and choose the correct answer.

1. What is the reading about?

    a. It's about a pizza.

    b. It's about the queen of pizza.

2. Where did Margherita pizza come from?

    a. Italy

    b. Canada

3. Margherita pizza is _____ after Queen Margherita.

    a. made   **b.** named

▪ Sentence Focus ▪

Read and choose the correct sentence.

1.
☐ King Margherita visited a pizzeria.
☐ Queen Margherita visited a pizzeria.

2.
☐ These days, Margherita pizza is for everyone.
☐ These days, Margherita pizza is only for kings and queens.

3.
☐ The baker used basil for green.
☐ The baker used tomatoes for green.

■ Word Practice ■

Look and complete the puzzle.

☀ Visualization   Story Elements

Use the words in the box to complete the chart.

    baker   loved

Who?		What?		Why?
The _____ in Naples	✛	He made a pizza of the Italian flag.	✛	The king and queen asked for a special pizza.
People	✛	They named the pizza Margherita pizza.	✛	The queen _____ the pizza.

UNIT 07
Ethics

We Are Friends

Talk About It 🎧

1 Look at the picture. How are they alike?

2 How are they different?

▪ Words to Know ▪

Listen and repeat. 🎧

feeling

pleasure

pain

friendly

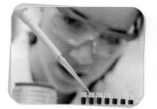

testing

down

circus

shark's fin

We Are Friends 🎧

We have feelings.
We feel pleasure.
We feel pain.

Just like us, animals have feelings.
Animals feel pleasure.
Animals feel pain.

Animals are our friends.

It's not friendly to use animals for testing shampoo.
It's not friendly to use animals for down pillows.
It's not friendly to use animals in the circus.
It's not friendly to use animals for shark's fin soup.

💬 **Key Expressions**
A : How are you and animals alike?
B : We have feelings.

▪ Comprehension Check ▪

Read and choose the correct answer.

1. **What is the reading about?**

   a. It's about how to make friends.

   b. It's about how animals are our friends.

2. **How are animals and people alike?**

   a. Both have feelings.

   b. Both use shampoo.

3. **Just like us, animals feel pleasure and _____.**

   a. friend   **b.** pain

▪ Sentence Focus ▪

Read and choose the correct sentence.

1.
   ☐ People have feelings.
   ☐ Animals have feelings.

2.
   ☐ Animals are our friends.
   ☐ Scientists are our friends.

3.
   ☐ It's not friendly to use animals in the circus.
   ☐ It's not friendly to use animals for down pillows.

▪ Word Practice ▪

Look and complete the puzzle.

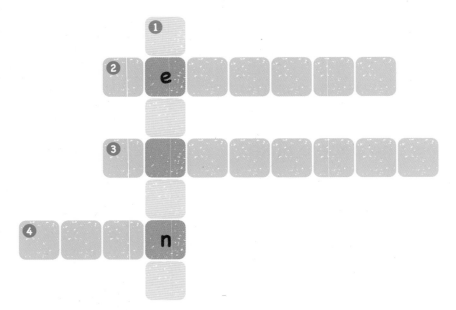

☀ Visualization   Author's Purpose

Use the words in the box to complete the chart.

> feelings   friendly

Fact 1

We have feelings.

Fact 2

Just like us, animals have _____.

It's not _____ to use animals for shark's fin soup or testing shampoo. Animals have rights!

Author's Purpose

38

Save the Tigers

Talk About It 🎧

1 Where are the tigers?
2 How are the two tigers alike and different?

· Words to Know ·

Listen and repeat. 🎧

biggest

tiger

weigh

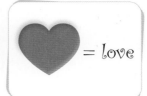

= love

symbol

power

hunt

bravery

extinct

Save the Tigers 🎧

The Biggest Cats

Tigers are the biggest cats in the world.
How much can one weigh?
A tiger can weigh up to 300 kg.

▲ tiger 305 kg   ▲ lion 249 kg   ▲ jaguar 120 kg   ▲ puma 103 kg   ▲ leopard 89 kg

Big Cats, Small Numbers

Tigers are a symbol of power. However, some people
think hunting them is also a sign of bravery.
Many tigers have become extinct in the last 30 years.

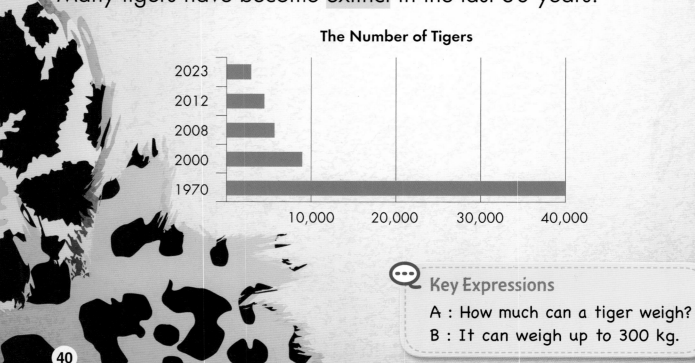

The Number of Tigers

Key Expressions

A : How much can a tiger weigh?
B : It can weigh up to 300 kg.

Comprehension Check

Read and choose the correct answer.

1. **What is the reading about?**

   a. It's about cats.

   b. It's about tigers.

2. **What do tigers symbolize?**

   a. extinction

   b. power

3. **The biggest cats in the world are _____.**

   a. tigers   **b.** leopards

Sentence Focus

Read and choose the correct sentence.

1.
   - ☐ A tiger can weigh up to 300 kg.
   - ☐ A puma can weigh up to 100 kg.

2.
   - ☐ Hunting tigers is a sign of bravery.
   - ☐ Hunting tigers is a sign of love.

3.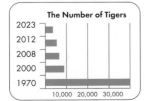
   - ☐ Many tigers have become powerful.
   - ☐ Many tigers have become extinct.

▪ Word Practice ▪

Look and complete the puzzle.

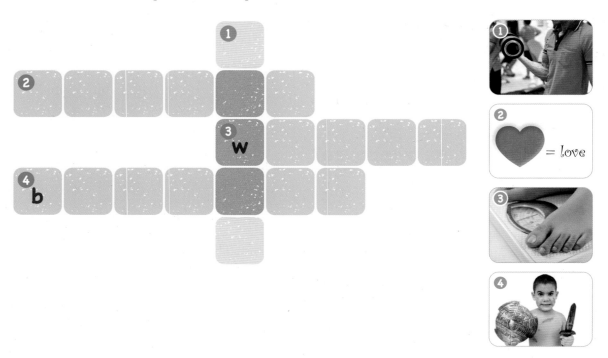

☀ Visualization Cause & Effect

Use the words in the box to complete the chart.

extinct   weigh   hunted

Why?		What Happened?
A tiger can _____ up to 300 kg.	⇒	Tigers are the biggest cats in the world.
People have _____ tigers.	⇒	Many tigers have become _____ .

Fly's First Flight

• Words to Know •

Listen and repeat. 🎧

flight

doorknob

air

fly

swing

ceiling

flap

wing

Fly's First Flight

"It's a great day for a flight!" said Fly's father.
So, Fly and his father went to the doorknob.
Fly's father went into the air. Zoom!
But, where's Fly?
"Fly! Come on, let's fly," said his father.
"No, no, I don't know how to fly.
I want to swing," said Fly.
Fly swung so high, he almost touched the ceiling.
He swung so high and Z-O-O-M!
He flew into the air.
"Help!" cried Fly.
"Flap your wings up and down!" cried his father.
Fly flapped his wings up and down really fast.
And you know what happened?
"Dad, I can fly!" sang Fly.
Now, Fly can fly.

Let's fly!

💬 **Key Expressions**

A : I don't know how to fly.
B : Flap your wings up and down.

44

▪ Comprehension Check ▪

Read and choose the correct answer.

1. **Who are the characters in the story?**

    a. Fly and his friends

    b. Fly and his father

2. **What problem does Fly have?**

    a. He doesn't know how to fly.

    b. He doesn't like to fly.

3. **Fly swings on the _____ .**

    a. ceiling   **b.** doorknob

▪ Sentence Focus ▪

Read and choose the correct sentence.

1.
    ☐ I want to go to the doorknob.
    ☐ I want to swing.

2.
    ☐ He almost touched the ceiling.
    ☐ He almost touched his father.

3.
    ☐ It flapped its wings up and down.
    ☐ It swung so high.

■ Word Practice ■

Look and complete the puzzle.

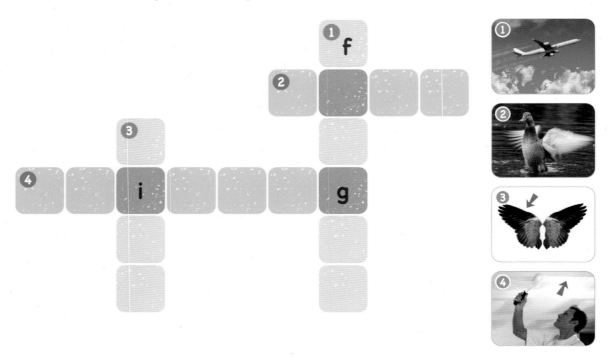

Visualization   Retell

Use the words in the box to complete the chart.

> air   fly

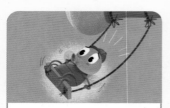

Fly swung
because he
didn't know how
to _____.

Fly swung so
high that he
flew into the
_____.

Fly flapped his
wings really
fast.
Now he can fly!

A Horrible Swimmer

Talk About It 🎧

1 Have you ever been to an aquarium?
2 What do you know about fish?

• Words to Know •

Listen and repeat. 🎧

strange

broad

slight

lipstick

lips

ocean floor

prefer

attack

A Horrible Swimmer 🎧

This red-lipped batfish looks strange.
It has a broad head and slight body.
It has a long nose-like fin.
It has red lipstick-like lips.
It has feet-like fins.

A red-lipped batfish can be found on the ocean floor.
It uses its feet-like fins for walking on the ocean floor.
It prefers walking to swimming.
It uses its long nose-like fin to attack small fish.
It can grow up to 40 cm long.

a long nose-like fin

red lipstick-like lips

feet-like fins

▲ red-lipped batfish resting
on the ocean floor

 Key Expressions

A : What do you know about
a red-lipped batfish?
B : It is a horrible swimmer.

Comprehension Check

Read and choose the correct answer.

1. What is the reading about?

   a. It's about the aquarium.

   b. It's about the red-lipped batfish.

2. How does a red-lipped batfish move?

   a. It swims above the ocean floor.

   b. It walks on the ocean floor.

3. A red-lipped batfish moves with its _____.

   a. lipstick-like lips   **b.** feet-like fins

Sentence Focus

Read and choose the correct sentence.

1.
  ☐ This red-lipped batfish looks like a starfish.
  ☐ This red-lipped batfish looks strange.

2.
  ☐ It has red lipstick-like lips.
  ☐ It has red lipstick-like fins.

3.
  ☐ It prefers walking to swimming.
  ☐ It prefers swimming to walking.

▪ Word Practice ▪

Look and complete the puzzle.

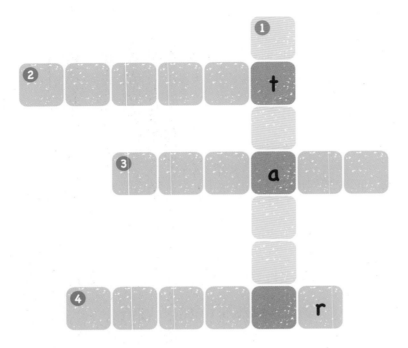

☼ Visualization Caption & Diagram

Use the words in the box to complete the chart.

> feet   lips

▲ This is a picture of
a red-lipped batfish.

a long nose-like fin:
attack small fish

red lipstick-like _____ :
look strange

_____-like fins:
walk on the ocean floor

50

Up

Talk About It 🎧

1 Do you like to go on picnics?
2 What do you like to pack in your picnic basket?

• Words to Know •

Listen and repeat. 🎧

hot-air balloon

basket

take off

scrape

treetop

higher

drop

steeple

Up 🎧

Three friends got in the hot-air balloon
basket with their picnic basket.
"Up we go!" they cried.
The hot-air balloon took off.

The hot-air balloon scraped the treetops.
"Can we go higher?" asked the sheep.
The donkey dropped one bag of sand.

The hot-air balloon scraped the rooftops.
"Can we go higher?" asked the pig.
The donkey dropped another bag of sand.

The hot-air balloon scraped the steeple.
"Can we go higher?" asked the sheep.
"There are no more bags of sand!" cried the pig.

Soon, the hot-air balloon went up
into the sky.
Do you know what the
donkey did?

💬 **Key Expressions**
A : Can we go higher?
B : Sure.

▪ Comprehension Check ▪

Read and choose the correct answer.

1. What is the story about?

   a. It's about a hot-air balloon race.

   b. It's about a hot-air balloon ride.

2. How did the hot-air balloon go up into the sky at the end?

   a. The donkey dropped a bag of sand.

   b. The donkey dropped the picnic basket.

3. Three friends are the donkey, _____, and the sheep.

   a. the cow   **b.** the pig

▪ Sentence Focus ▪

Read and choose the correct sentence.

1.
   ☐ Three friends got in the hot-air balloon basket.
   ☐ Three friends got in the picnic basket.

2.
   ☐ The hot-air balloon scraped the treetops.
   ☐ The hot-air balloon scraped the rooftops.

3.
   ☐ The hot-air balloon arrived.
   ☐ The hot-air balloon took off.

• Word Practice •

Look and complete the puzzle.

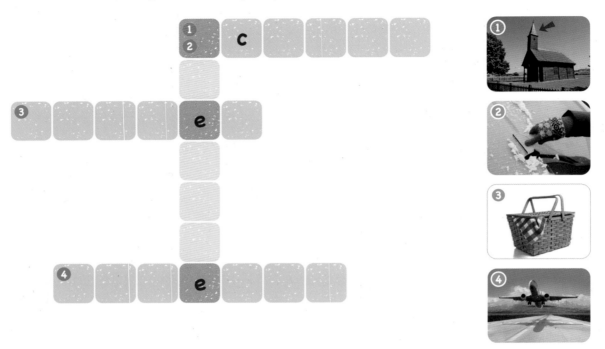

Visualization   Characters

Use the words in the box to complete the chart.

higher   dropped   higher

Characters		What Did They Do?
the sheep	→	asked the donkey to go up _____
the pig	→	asked the donkey to go up _____
the donkey	→	_____ their picnic basket to go up into the sky

Energy

Talk About It 🎧

1 How do people use energy?
2 Where do people get energy?

• Words to Know •

Listen and repeat. 🎧

talk

think

resource

electricity

heat

charge

cell phone

basketball

Energy

We use energy all the time.
We use energy when we walk.
We use energy when we talk.
We use energy when we think.
We even use energy when we sleep.

We get energy from many different resources.
We get energy from the sun, wind,
electricity and food.

We can use the sun's energy to heat buildings.
We can use wind to sail a boat.
We use electricity to charge cell phones.
When we get energy from food,
we can play basketball.

Key Expressions

A : What can you do with
    energy?
B : I can use energy to think.

▪ Comprehension Check ▪

Read and choose the correct answer.

1. **What is the reading about?**

    a. It's about how we use energy.

    b. It's about how we use cell phones.

2. **When do we use energy?**

    a. We use energy all the time.

    b. We use energy only when we play.

3. **We get energy from the _____.**

    a. basketball   **b.** sun

▪ Sentence Focus ▪

Read and choose the correct sentence.

1.
    ☐ We use energy when we talk.
    ☐ We use energy when we think.

2.
    ☐ We get energy from food.
    ☐ We get energy from electricity.

3.
    ☐ We use wind to fly a kite.
    ☐ We use wind to sail a boat.

Word Practice

Look and complete the puzzle.

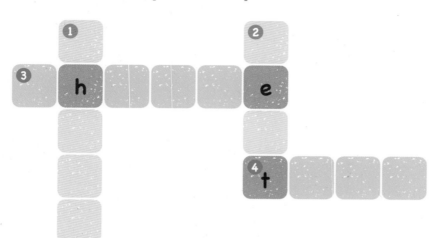

Visualization   Cause & Effect

Use the words in the box to complete the chart.

charge   talk

Why?		What Happened?
We get energy from food.		We can walk, _____, play and think.
We _____ cell phones with electricity.		We can use cell phones.

Not Impossible

Talk About It 🎧

1 What do you think about this man?
2 Do you think it's possible to help him? Why or why not?

• Words to Know •

Listen and repeat. 🎧

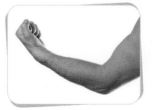

arm

blow off

bombing

travel

3-D printer

teach

village

Sudanese

Not Impossible 🎧

Mick read about a boy.
The boy's name was Daniel.
Daniel lived in Sudan.
Daniel's arms were blown off
during a bombing.
Mick thought Daniel needed help.
He thought he could do something for Daniel.

Mick traveled to Sudan.
He used a 3-D printer to make
arms for Daniel.
He taught the village how to
make arms.
He gave the village his computer
and 3-D printer.

Now, the village can help other Sudanese.
The village can make arms for them.

> **Key Expressions**
> A : How can you help Daniel?
> B : I can use a 3-D printer
> to make arms for Daniel.

▪ Comprehension Check ▪

Read and choose the correct answer.

1. **What is the story about?**

   a. It's about Daniel.

   b. It's about Sudan.

2. **How did Mick help Daniel?**

   a. Mick gave Daniel his 3-D printer.

   b. Mick made arms for Daniel.

3. **Mick _____ the village to help other Sudanese.**

   a. gave   **b.** taught

▪ Sentence Focus ▪

Read and choose the correct sentence.

1.
   ☐ He read about a boy.
   ☐ He talked about a boy.

2.
   ☐ She traveled to Sudan.
   ☐ She lived in Sudan.

3.
   ☐ He used a 3-D printer to make arms.
   ☐ He used a 3-D printer to go to Sudan.

▪ Word Practice ▪

Look and complete the puzzle.

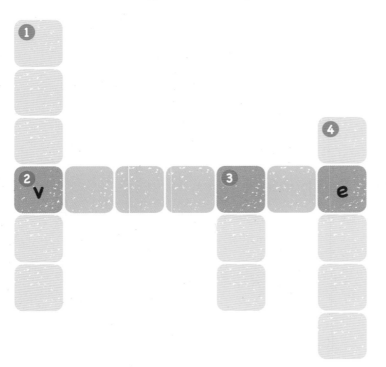

💡 Visualization   Draw a Conclusion

Use the words in the box to complete the chart.

bombing   Sudanese

Fact 1

Daniel's arms were blown off during a _____ .

Fact 2

Mick used a 3-D printer to make arms for Daniel.

Other _____ like Daniel can have new arms. It is not impossible!

Conclusion

62

Technology

CHAT APPS EMAIL TIME MANAGEMENT DISCOVER FUN RESTAURANT LOCATION Gallery Restaurant PLAY SERVICES ENTERTAINMENT VIDEO INTERNET WORK FINANCES MUSIC INSTRUMENTS

Talk About It 🎧

1 What is technology?
2 What technologies do you use every day?

• Words to Know •

Listen and repeat. 🎧

technology

life

easier

healthier

bring

closer

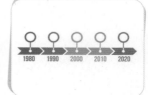

timeline

change

Technology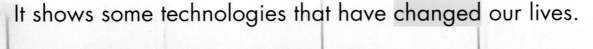

Technology has made our lives easier.
Technology has made our lives healthier.
Technology has made our lives fun.
And it has also helped bring people closer together.

Look at the timeline.
It shows some technologies that have changed our lives.

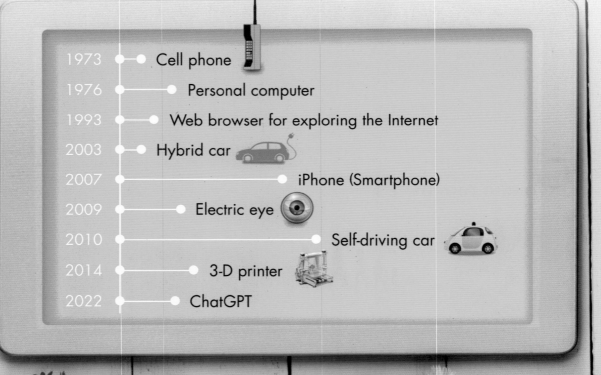

1973	Cell phone
1976	Personal computer
1993	Web browser for exploring the Internet
2003	Hybrid car
2007	iPhone (Smartphone)
2009	Electric eye
2010	Self-driving car
2014	3-D printer
2022	ChatGPT

Key Expressions

A : How have technologies changed our lives?

B : They have made our lives fun.

▪ Comprehension Check ▪

Read and choose the correct answer.

1. What is the reading about?

   a. It's about what technology is.

   b. It's about how technology has changed our lives.

2. When did the 3-D printer come out?

   a. 2009

   b. 2014

3. ChatGPT came out _____ cell phones.

   a. before   **b.** after

▪ Sentence Focus ▪

Read and choose the correct sentence.

1.
  ☐ Technology has made our lives boring.
  ☐ Technology has made our lives fun.

2.
  ☐ Technology has made our lives healthier.
  ☐ Technology has not changed our lives.

3.
  ☐ These show some technologies.
  ☐ These show some timelines.

▪ Word Practice ▪

Look and complete the puzzle.

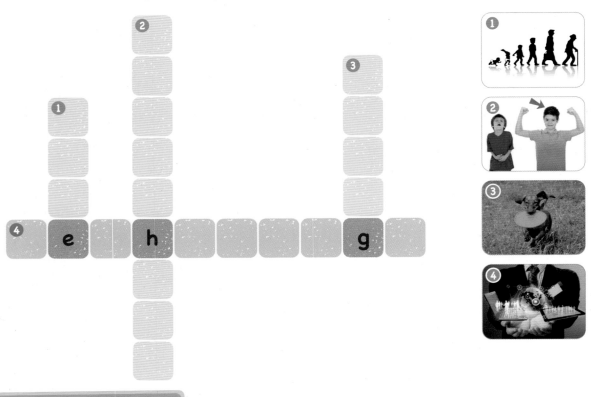

🔆 Visualization Main Idea & Details

Use the words in the box to complete the chart.

Technology   closer

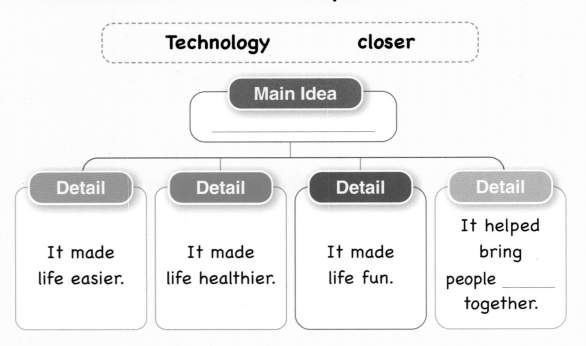

3-D Movies

Talk About It

1 Do you like movies?
2 What's your favorite movie?

· Words to Know ·

Listen and repeat.

movie

Friday

favorite

first

experience

lab

burst

3-D glasses

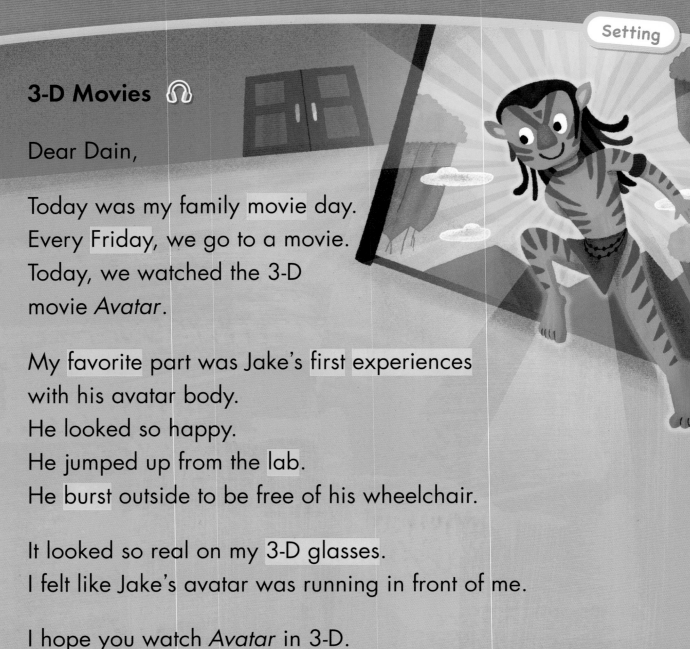

3-D Movies 🎧

Dear Dain,

Today was my family movie day.
Every Friday, we go to a movie.
Today, we watched the 3-D
movie *Avatar*.

My favorite part was Jake's first experiences
with his avatar body.
He looked so happy.
He jumped up from the lab.
He burst outside to be free of his wheelchair.

It looked so real on my 3-D glasses.
I felt like Jake's avatar was running in front of me.

I hope you watch *Avatar* in 3-D.

Love,
Sue

Key Expressions
A : What did you do yesterday?
B : It was my family movie day.

▪ Comprehension Check ▪

Read and choose the correct answer.

1. **What am I doing?**

   a. I am talking with Dain.

   b. I am writing an e-mail.

2. **When does my family go to a movie?**

   a. every Friday

   b. every day

3. **I like to watch 3-D _____ because they look real.**

   a. glasses   **b.** movies

▪ Sentence Focus ▪

Read and choose the correct sentence.

1.

   ☐ Every Friday, we go to a movie.
   ☐ Every Friday, we go to the lab.

2.

   ☐ This is my favorite part of the movie.
   ☐ This is my favorite part of the book.

3.

   ☐ It looks so real on my 3-D glasses.
   ☐ It looks so sad on my 3-D glasses.

▪ Word Practice ▪

Look and complete the puzzle.

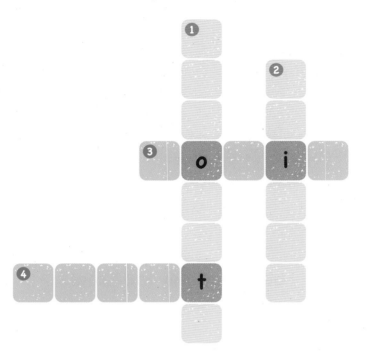

☼ Visualization   Setting

Use the words in the box to complete the chart.

┌───┐
│   3-D glasses   Friday   │
└───┘

When?

_____

Where?

at the theater

What?

· We watched a 3-D movie.

· We wore _____.

· It looked so real.

70

Social Media

Talk About It 🎧

1 Do you have a smartphone?
2 When do you use your smartphone?

• Words to Know •

Listen and repeat. 🎧

learn

connected

share

funny

use

topic

information

free

Social Media 🎧

You can use your social media every day.

You can stay connected with friends and family members.
You can share funny videos and photos.
You can chat online about any topic you like.
You can share information with others and learn from them.
This means you can do better in school.
Moreover, most of it is free!

Social media can be good for you.
Enjoy your social media!

💬 **Key Expressions**

A : What can you do with
    social media?
B : I can share funny videos.

Comprehension Check

Read and choose the correct answer.

1. **What is the reading about?**

   a. It's about how to make social media.

   b. It's about what you can do with social media.

2. **What can you do with social media?**

   a. I can share photos with my friends.

   b. I can share toys with my friends.

3. **Most social media is _____.**

   a. better   **b.** free

Sentence Focus

Read and choose the correct sentence.

1. ☐ You can use your social media every day.
   ☐ You can buy your social media every day.

2. ☐ I can share my topics.
   ☐ I can share my videos.

3. ☐ You can do better in school.
   ☐ You can do better in social media.

Word Practice

Look and complete the puzzle.

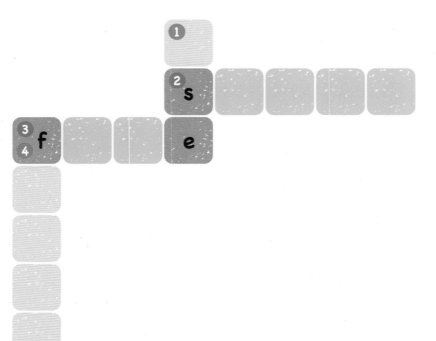

Visualization Cause & Effect

Use the words in the box to complete the chart.

connected   learn

Why?		What Happened?
Social media can be good for you.		You stay _____ with others.
Social media can help you do better in school.		You _____ from social media about any topic.

Raise Money

Talk About It 🎧

1 Have you ever raised money?
2 Do you have any ideas to raise money?

▪ Words to Know ▪

Listen and repeat. 🎧

raise money

broken

wrapping papers

sell

cheap

expensive

buy

price

Raise Money

Leo and Sue are thinking about
ways to raise money.

"Why don't we wash cars?"
"Good idea. But you have a broken leg!"
"Why don't we sell old toys?"
"Cool idea!"

"How about 1,000 won for a toy?"
"That's too cheap.
We need to buy wrapping papers and ribbons.
That's already 1,000 won."
"How about 5,000 won for a toy?"
"That's too expensive.
No one will buy our toys."
"You're right!
Let's think carefully about the price."
"All right!"

Key Expressions
A : How can you raise money?
B : I can sell old toys.

Comprehension Check

Read and choose the correct answer.

1. **Who is thinking about ways to raise money?**

   a. Leo and his mom

   b. Leo and Sue

2. **What will Leo and Sue do to raise money?**

   a. They will wash cars.

   b. They will sell old toys.

3. **Leo and Sue need to think carefully about the _____ .**

   a. price   b. cars

Sentence Focus

Read and choose the correct sentence.

1.
   ☐ That's 1,000 won.
   ☐ That's 5,000 won.

2.
   ☐ We need to buy wrapping papers.
   ☐ We need to buy ribbons.

3.
   ☐ How about 1,000 won for a toy?
   ☐ How about 2,000 won for a toy?

▪ Word Practice ▪

Look and complete the puzzle.

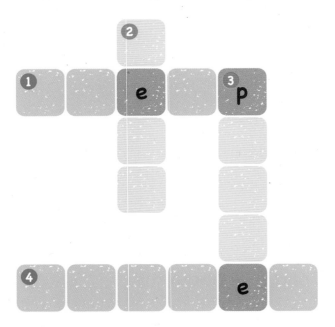

☼ Visualization Main Idea & Details

Use the words in the box to complete the chart.

expensive   sell

Main Idea

Raise Money

Detail

· Kids can wash cars.
· Kids can _____ old toys.

Detail

· The price should not be too cheap.
· The price should not be too _____.

History of Money

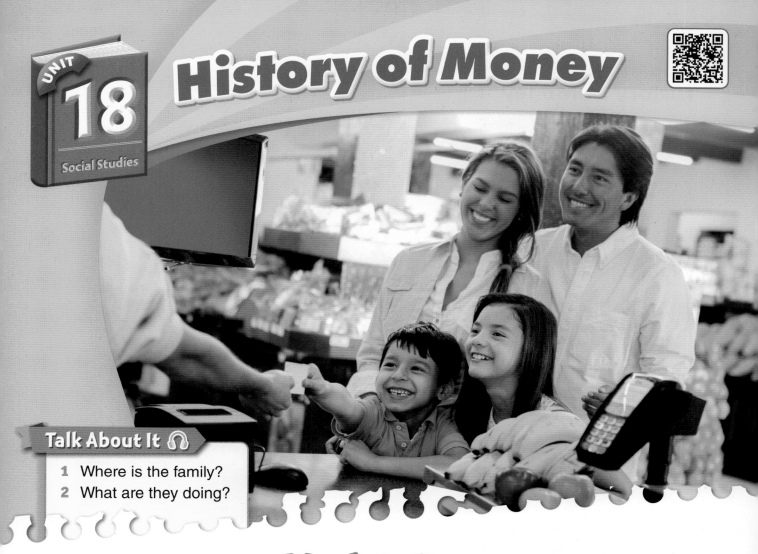

Talk About It

1 Where is the family?
2 What are they doing?

• Words to Know •

Listen and repeat.

swap

without

paper money

coin

credit card

invent

payment

invisible

History of Money 🎧

Swapping
People lived without money in 9000 B.C.
Instead of money, people swapped things.

First Money
Three thousand years ago, people used shells for money.
Instead of swapping things, people bought
things with shells.

Money
People started to use paper money and
coins to buy things.

Credit Cards
The credit card was invented in the 1950s.
People didn't need to carry money any more.

Online Payments
Today, most money in the world is invisible.

💬 **Key Expressions**
A : How did you pay for your iPad?
B : I made an online payment.

▪ Comprehension Check ▪

Read and choose the correct answer.

1. What is the reading about?

   a. It's about the history of money.

   b. It's about the history of technology.

2. How do most people pay for things these days?

   a. by swapping

   b. by online payments

3. _____ were used as the first money.

   a. Credit cards   **b.** Shells

▪ Sentence Focus ▪

Read and choose the correct sentence.

1.
  ☐ People swapped things instead of money.
  ☐ People used shells for money.

2.
  ☐ The credit card was invented in the 1950s.
  ☐ The online payment was made in the 1950s.

3.
  ☐ Today, most money in the world is invisible.
  ☐ Today, most money in the world is heavy.

▪ Word Practice ▪

Look and complete the puzzle.

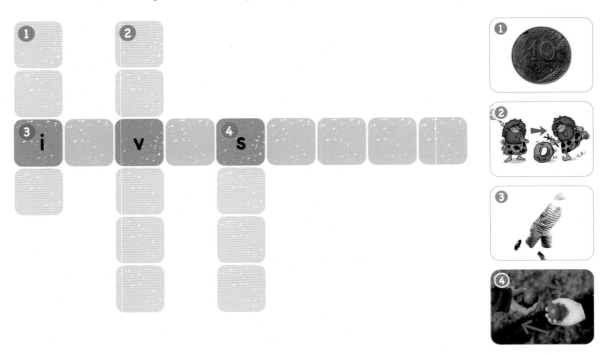

☼ Visualization   Sequence

Use the words in the box to complete the chart.

carry   shells

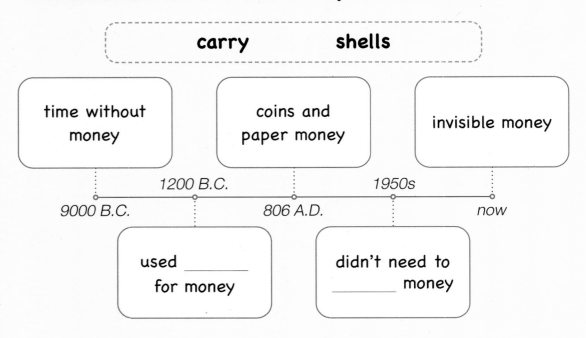

time without money   coins and paper money   invisible money

1200 B.C.   1950s

9000 B.C.   806 A.D.   now

used _____ for money

didn't need to _____ money

Matt's Pancakes

Talk About It 🎧

1 Are you hungry?
2 What do you want to eat?

▪ Words to Know ▪

Listen and repeat. 🎧

recipe

mix

flour

bowl

beat

combine

spread

top

Matt's Pancakes 🎧

Matt is feeling hungry.
He thinks of some pancakes.
He has never made pancakes before.
He looks inside his mom's big recipe book.

He mixes some flour and the baking
powder in a bowl.
Next, he beats eggs in another bowl.
Then, he adds sugar and milk.
Last, he combines the egg mixture and the
flour mixture.
He spreads the mixture in a pan
and bakes for three minutes.
Now, the pancake is ready!

He tops his pancake with
ice cream.
Gulp, yum!

Matt loves his first pancake!

3 Minutes

💬 **Key Expressions**

A : Do you know how to make
pancakes?

B : Yes.

▪ Comprehension Check ▪

Read and choose the correct answer.

1. What is the reading about?

   a. It's about how to make pancakes.

   b. It's about why Matt loves pancakes.

2. Why does Matt look inside his mom's recipe book?

   a. Because he has never made pancakes before.

   b. Because he loves his mom's pancake recipe.

3. Matt loves his _____ pancake!

   a. first   **b.** last

▪ Sentence Focus ▪

Read and choose the correct sentence.

1.
☐ He beats eggs in a bowl.
☐ He beats eggs in a pan.

2.
☐ He spreads the jam on the bread.
☐ He bakes the mixture in a pan.

3.
☐ He tops his pancake with cocoa.
☐ He tops his pancake with ice cream.

▪ Word Practice ▪

Look and complete the puzzle.

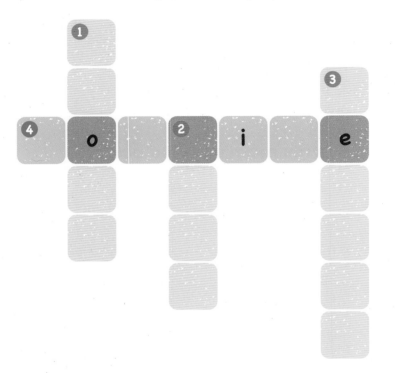

☼ Visualization   Retell

Use the words in the box to complete the chart.

> recipe   tops

Why?		What?
Matt is feeling hungry.	➡	· Matt looks inside his mom's _____ book. · He bakes a pancake. · He _____ his pancake with ice cream.

Kitchen Chemistry

UNIT 20 · Science

Talk About It 🎧

1 What is the boy doing?
2 What are three states of matter?

· Words to Know ·

Listen and repeat. 🎧

science

chemical reaction

plate

drop

food coloring

cotton swab

liquid

stir

Kitchen Chemistry

Chemistry is a type of science.
It is about how matter changes.
A chemical reaction happens when matter changes.

Pour some milk in a plate.
Add one drop each of four different
colors of food coloring.
Find a clean cotton swab.
Place a drop of liquid dish soap
on the cotton swab.
It's important not to stir the milk.
Just touch it with the cotton swab.
What happened?
A beautiful picture appeared on the surface of the milk.
This is chemistry.

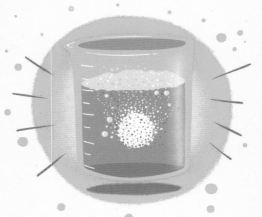

▲ a chemical reaction

Key Expressions
A : What is chemistry?
B : It's about how matter changes.

Comprehension Check

Read and choose the correct answer.

1. **What is the reading about?**

    a. It's about bathroom chemistry.

    b. It's about kitchen chemistry.

2. **What is chemistry?**

    a. It is about what matter is.

    b. It is about how matter changes.

3. **In the picture, the _____ are a chemical reaction.**

    a. bubbles   **b.** plates

Sentence Focus

Read and choose the correct sentence.

1.

    ☐ Chemistry is a type of art.

    ☐ Chemistry is a type of science.

2.

    ☐ Add one drop of food coloring.

    ☐ Pour a cup of food coloring.

3.

    ☐ It is important to stir the milk.

    ☐ It is important not to stir the milk.

■ Word Practice ■

Look and complete the puzzle.

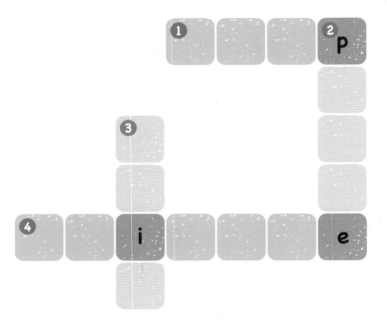

☀ Visualization | Cause & Effect

Use the words in the box to complete the chart.

Cause		Effect
Matter changes.	→	A chemical _____ takes place.
You combined milk, food coloring, and _____ dish soap.	→	A beautiful picture appeared.

UNIT 01

☐	**costume**	의상
☐	**scream**	소리 지르다
☐	**scary**	무서운
☐	**treat**	간식
☐	**ghost**	유령
☐	**witch**	마녀
☐	**howl**	(길게) 울다
☐	**skeleton**	해골

UNIT 02

☐	**laser**	레이저
☐	**maze**	미로
☐	**hallway**	복도
☐	**crepe paper**	주름종이
☐	**navigate**	길을 찾다
☐	**adjust**	조절하다
☐	**stopwatch**	스톱워치
☐	**player**	선수

UNIT 03

☐	**baseball**	야구
☐	**enter**	들어가다
☐	**score**	점수
☐	**tie**	동점
☐	**home plate**	본루
☐	**pitch**	투구
☐	**strike**	스트라이크
☐	**swing**	휘두르다

UNIT 04

☐	**mother**	어머니
☐	**father**	아버지
☐	**member**	구성원
☐	**feed**	먹이를 주다
☐	**guitar**	기타
☐	**family**	가족
☐	**have fun**	즐겁게 지내다
☐	**hide-and-seek**	숨바꼭질

UNIT 05

☐	**build**	짓다
☐	**treehouse**	나무 위의 집
☐	**wood**	목재
☐	**nail**	못을 박다
☐	**trunk**	나무의 몸통
☐	**climb**	오르다
☐	**board**	널빤지
☐	**order**	주문하다

UNIT 06

☐	**Italy**	이탈리아
☐	**king**	왕
☐	**visit**	방문하다
☐	**pizzeria**	피자 가게
☐	**baker**	제빵사
☐	**Italian flag**	이탈리아 국기
☐	**basil**	바질
☐	**everyone**	모든 사람

UNIT 07

☐	**feeling**	감정
☐	**pleasure**	기쁨
☐	**pain**	고통
☐	**friendly**	친절한
☐	**testing**	실험
☐	**down**	(새의) 부드러운 털
☐	**circus**	서커스
☐	**shark's fin**	상어 지느러미

UNIT 08

☐	**biggest**	가장 큰
☐	**tiger**	호랑이
☐	**weigh**	무게가 나가다
☐	**symbol**	상징
☐	**power**	힘
☐	**hunt**	사냥하다
☐	**bravery**	용기
☐	**extinct**	멸종된

UNIT 09

☐	**flight**	비행
☐	**doorknob**	(문의) 손잡이
☐	**air**	공중
☐	**fly**	날다
☐	**swing**	그네를 타다
☐	**ceiling**	천장
☐	**flap**	(날개를) 퍼덕거리다
☐	**wing**	날개

UNIT 10

☐	**strange**	이상한
☐	**broad**	넓은
☐	**slight**	작고 여윈, 갸날픈
☐	**lipstick**	립스틱
☐	**lips**	입술
☐	**ocean floor**	해저
☐	**prefer**	선호하다
☐	**attack**	공격하다

UNIT 11

- [ ] hot-air balloon — 열기구
- [ ] basket — 바구니
- [ ] take off — 이륙하다
- [ ] scrape — 긁다
- [ ] treetop — 나무 꼭대기
- [ ] higher — 더 높이
- [ ] drop — 떨어뜨리다
- [ ] steeple — 뾰족탑

UNIT 12

- [ ] talk — 말하다
- [ ] think — 생각하다
- [ ] resource — 자원
- [ ] electricity — 전기
- [ ] heat — 따뜻하게 만들다
- [ ] charge — 충전하다
- [ ] cell phone — 휴대폰
- [ ] basketball — 농구

UNIT 13

- [ ] arm — 팔
- [ ] blow off — (폭탄으로) 날려 버리다
- [ ] bombing — 폭격
- [ ] travel — 여행하다
- [ ] 3-D printer — 3D 프린터
- [ ] teach — 가르치다
- [ ] village — 마을, 마을 사람들
- [ ] Sudanese — 수단 사람

UNIT 14

- [ ] technology — 기술
- [ ] life — 삶
- [ ] easier — 더 쉬운
- [ ] healthier — 더 건강한
- [ ] bring — 가져오다
- [ ] closer — 더 가까운
- [ ] timeline — 연대표
- [ ] change — 바꾸다

UNIT 15

- [ ] movie — 영화
- [ ] Friday — 금요일
- [ ] favorite — 가장 좋아하는
- [ ] first — 첫 번째의
- [ ] experience — 경험
- [ ] lab — 실험실
- [ ] burst — 불쑥 나오다
- [ ] 3-D glasses — 3D 안경

UNIT 16

- [ ] learn — 배우다
- [ ] connected — 연결된
- [ ] share — 공유하다
- [ ] funny — 재미있는
- [ ] use — 사용하다
- [ ] topic — 주제
- [ ] information — 정보
- [ ] free — 무료의

UNIT 17

☐	raise money	(용)돈을 마련하다
☐	broken	부러진
☐	wrapping papers	포장지
☐	sell	팔다
☐	cheap	(값이) 싼
☐	expensive	(값이) 비싼
☐	buy	사다
☐	price	값

UNIT 18

☐	swap	교환하다
☐	without	~ 없이
☐	paper money	지폐
☐	coin	동전
☐	credit card	신용카드
☐	invent	발명하다
☐	payment	지불
☐	invisible	눈에 보이지 않는

UNIT 19

☐	recipe	조리법
☐	mix	섞다
☐	flour	밀가루
☐	bowl	그릇
☐	beat	휘저어 섞다
☐	combine	결합시키다
☐	spread	바르다
☐	top	위에 올리다

UNIT 20

☐	science	과학
☐	chemical reaction	화학반응
☐	plate	접시
☐	drop	방울
☐	food coloring	식용색소
☐	cotton swab	면봉
☐	liquid	액체의
☐	stir	휘젓다

단어 블록 연결로
초등 **문법**과 **영작**을 동시에 해결!

기적의 영어문장 만들기 **①~⑤**

주선이 지음 | 각 권 14,000원 | 초등 4~5학년 대상

1. 재미있는 역할극 만화로 문법 개념을 쉽게 이해해요.

2. 단어 블록을 조합하여 문장 어순을 한눈에 파악해요.

3. 뼈대 문장부터 긴 문장까지 단계적으로 직접 써 보며 훈련해요.

☆👆 **추천 대상**

☑ 단어는 많이 알지만 문장 완성은 자신이 없는 학생

☑ 주어나 시제에 따른 동사 사용에 실수가 많은 학생

☑ 고학년 대비 기초 문법을 익히고 싶은 학생

길벗스쿨

리딩 첫걸음부터 완성까지!
초등학생의 영어 성장을 이끄는 4단계 리딩 프로그램

기적의 영어리딩

7세~초등 1학년   **초등 2~3학년**   **초등 4~5학년**   **초등 6학년 이상**

E2K 지음 | 30, 50 단계 각 권 13,000원 | 80, 120 단계 각 권 14,000원

단계	대상	특징	지문당 단어수
기적의 영어리딩 30 (전 3권)	7세~초등 1학년	패턴 문장으로 탄탄한 기초 실력 쌓기	30~40 단어
기적의 영어리딩 50 (전 3권)	초등 2~3학년		50~60 단어
기적의 영어리딩 80 (전 2권)	초등 4~5학년	끊어읽기 연습으로 정확한 독해 완성하기	70~80 단어
기적의 영어리딩 120 (전 2권)	초등 6학년 이상		120~130 단어

교재 특징

1 패턴 문장으로 리딩 첫걸음을 쉽게, 끊어 읽기 연습으로 직독직해 능력 향상!

2 초등 필수 어휘는 물론 리딩 빈출 어휘까지 완벽히 습득

3 워크북과 다양한 부가자료를 활용하여 꼼꼼하고 철저한 복습 가능

길벗스쿨

2.3

미국교과서 리딩

READING

Workbook & Answer Key

길벗스쿨

미국교과서 리딩

READING

LEVEL 2 ③

Workbook

길벗스쿨

Scary Night

Word Review

A Choose and write.

| witch | howl | costume | skeleton | ghost | treat |

1.

costume

2.

3.

4.

5.

6.

B Read and choose.

1. We tell <u>scary</u> stories.

   ⓑ

2. We scream real loud.

ⓐ ⓑ

Sentence Review

A **Read and match.**

1. We eat

2. We walk

3. We howl like

a. like a ghost.

b. lots of treats.

c. a wolf man.

B **Unscramble and write.**

1. at Ben's.   have   We   a sleepover party

→ We have a sleepover party at Ben's.

2. like   fly   We   a witch.

→

3. like   shake   We   a skeleton.

→

UNIT 02

The Laser Maze

Word Review

A **Choose and write.**

| adjust | maze | navigate | player | laser | stopwatch |

1. _____

2. _____

3. _____

4. _____

5. _____

6. _____

B **Read and choose.**

1. Cut strips of crepe paper.

    ☐

2. Make a laser maze in the hallway.

    ☐

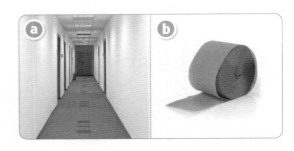

Sentence Review

A **Read and match.**

1. Tape strips all

2. Adjust

3. The players may not

a   along the hallway.

b   the laser maze.

c   touch the maze strips.

B **Unscramble and write.**

1. maze.   Make   a laser

   →

2. The fastest   wins   player   the game.

   →

3. through   the laser maze.   Each player   navigates

   →

My Best Birthday

Word Review

A **Choose and write.**

| enter | score | strike | swing | pitch | home plate |

1.

_____
- - - - - - - - - - - -

2.

_____
- - - - - - - - - - - -

3.

_____
- - - - - - - - - - - -

4.

_____
- - - - - - - - - - - -

5.

_____
- - - - - - - - - - - -

6.

_____
- - - - - - - - - - - -

B **Read and choose.**

1. Dad took me out to a baseball game.

2. The score was a tie.

Sentence Review

A) Read and match.

1. The batter swung

2. The Bears entered

3. The first pitch

a. hard and CRACK!

b. was a fastball.

c. the stadium.

B) Unscramble and write.

1. cheered | We | for | the home team.

→

2. home plate. | stood | The batter | at

→

3. It | my | was | ever! | best birthday

→

We Love and Care

Word Review

Ⓐ Choose and write.

| guitar | member | feed | mother | father | have fun |

1.
_____

2.
_____

3.
_____

4.
_____

5.
_____

6.
_____

Ⓑ Read and choose.

1. Family members love each other. ☐

2. Vera plays hide-and-seek with her mother. ☐

Sentence Review

A **Read and match.**

1. Families can be

2. Family members

3. John bakes a

a cake with his father.

b help each other.

c very different.

B **Unscramble and write.**

1. | have fun | together. | Family members |

   →

2. | Amy's mother | to play | teaches | the guitar. | Amy |

   →

3. | his father | the dog. | helps | Nate | by feeding |

   →

UNIT 05

The Treehouse

Word Review

A Choose and write.

| build | board | trunk | order | nail | climb |

1.

_____

2.

_____

3.

_____

4.

_____

5.

_____

6.

_____

B Read and choose.

1. We cut some <u>wood</u>.
   ☐

2. I'm going to build a <u>treehouse</u>.
   ☐

Sentence Review

A **Read and match.**

1. What do you want

2. It's cool to eat pizza

3. We nail the wood for

a. in my treehouse.

b. to do now?

c. the floor.

B **Unscramble and write.**

1. some   order   Let's   pizza!

→

2. can do   I   in it.   cool things   lots of

→

3. the board   put up   We   for the roof.

→

Pizza for Kings and Queens

Word Review

A Choose and write.

| king | visit | baker | basil | pizzeria | Italian flag |

1.

_____

2.

_____

3.

_____

4.

_____

5.

_____

6.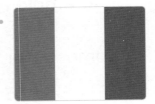

_____

B Read and choose.

1. It's for everyone.
☐

2. Margherita pizza came from Italy.
☐

Sentence Review

A **Read and match.**

1. The king and queen

2. It was named

3. He used basil

a. after Queen Margherita.

b. for green.

c. went to a pizzeria.

B **Unscramble and write.**

1. | made | The baker | a pizza | of the Italian flag. |

   →

2. | for red. | He | tomatoes | used |

   →

3. | loved | The king | it. | and queen |

   →

UNIT 07
We Are Friends

Word Review

A **Choose and write.**

testing	pleasure	friendly	down	circus	shark's fin

1.

_ _ _ _ _ _ _ _ _ _ _ _ _ _ _ _

2.

_ _ _ _ _ _ _ _ _ _ _ _ _ _ _ _

3.

_ _ _ _ _ _ _ _ _ _ _ _ _ _ _ _

4.

_ _ _ _ _ _ _ _ _ _ _ _ _ _ _ _

5.

_ _ _ _ _ _ _ _ _ _ _ _ _ _ _ _

6.

_ _ _ _ _ _ _ _ _ _ _ _ _ _ _ _

B **Read and choose.**

1. We feel pain.

2. We have feelings.

Sentence Review

A **Read and match.**

1. Animals feel

2. Animals are

3. It's not friendly to

a. use animals in the circus.

b. our friends.

c. pain.

B **Unscramble and write.**

1. feel | pleasure. | We

2. Just like | have | animals | us, | feelings.

3. not friendly | to use | It's | for testing shampoo. | animals

UNIT 08 Save the Tigers

Word Review

A Choose and write.

bravery	power	symbol	extinct	biggest	weigh

1.

_____

2.

_____

3.

_____

4.

_____

5.

_____

6.

_____

B Read and choose.

1. A tiger can weigh up to 300 kg.
   ☐

2. Hunting them is also a sign of bravery.
   ☐

 ⓐ

 ⓑ

Sentence Review

A **Read and match.**

1. How much

2. Tigers are the biggest

3. Tigers are a

a. cats in the world.

b. can one weigh?

c. symbol of power.

B **Unscramble and write.**

1. can | How much | a tiger | weigh?

→

2. A jaguar | can weigh | 120 kg. | up to

→

3. Many tigers | extinct. | have become

→

Fly's First Flight

Word Review

A Choose and write.

| flight | ceiling | air | fly | flap | wing |

1.

_____

2.

_____

3.

_____

4.

_____

5.

_____

6.

_____

B Read and choose.

1. Fly and his father went to the <u>doorknob</u>. ☐

2. I want to <u>swing</u>. ☐

Sentence Review

A **Read and match.**

1. It's a great day

2. I don't know

3. Flap your wings

a for a flight!

b how to fly.

c up and down!

B **Unscramble and write.**

1. | Fly's father | into | went | the air. |

   →

2. | touched | almost | He | the ceiling. |

   →

3. | Fly | his wings | flapped | up and down | really fast. |

   →

A Horrible Swimmer

Word Review

A Choose and write.

strange	prefer	lipstick	slight	broad	lips

1.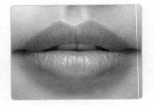

_____

2.

_____

3.

_____

4.

_____

5.

_____

6.

_____

B Read and choose.

1. It can be found on the <u>ocean floor</u>.

   ☐

2. It uses its long fin to <u>attack</u> small fish.

   ☐

Sentence Review

A **Read and match.**

1. A red-lipped batfish

2. It has a long

3. It can grow

a up to 40 cm long.

b looks strange.

c nose-like fin.

B **Unscramble and write.**

1. It | walking | swimming. | to | prefers

→

2. lipstick-like | has | It | red | lips.

→

3. It | swimmer. | a horrible | is

→

11 Up

Word Review

A Choose and write.

| basket | treetop | drop | scrape | steeple | take off |

1.
_____

2.
_____

3.
_____

4.
_____

5.
_____

6.
_____

B Read and choose.

1. Can we go higher? ☐

2. The hot-air balloon took off. ☐

Sentence Review

A **Read and match.**

1. The hot-air balloon

2. The donkey dropped

3. Do you know

a) scraped the rooftops.

b) what the donkey did?

c) one bag of sand.

B **Unscramble and write.**

1. The hot-air balloon   the treetops.   scraped

2. are   no more   There   bags of sand!

3. the hot-air balloon   into   went up   the sky.   Soon,

Energy

Word Review

A **Choose and write.**

| charge | think | electricity | cell phone | resource | heat |

1.

_____
_____

2.

_____
_____

3.

_____
_____

4.

_____
_____

5.

_____
_____

6.

_____
_____

B **Read and choose.**

1. We can play basketball. ☐

2. We use energy when we talk. ☐

Sentence Review

A **Read and match.**

1. We use energy when

2. We get energy from

3. We can use wind

a. many different resources.

b. we think.

c. to sail a boat.

B **Unscramble and write.**

1. | use | all the time. | We | energy |

→

2. | electricity | We | to charge | use | cell phones. |

→

3. | get | We | energy | from the sun, | and food. | wind, |

→

UNIT 13 Not Impossible

Word Review

A Choose and write.

| 3-D printer   teach   village   arm   Sudanese   blow off |

1.

_____

2.

_____

3.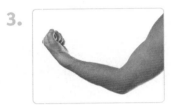

_____

4.

_____

5.

_____

6.

_____

B Read and choose.

1. Mick traveled to Sudan.

   [ ]

2. Daniel's arms were blown off during a bombing.

   [ ]

Sentence Review

A **Read and match.**

1. The boy's name

2. He taught the village

3. Now, the village can

a. help other Sudanese.

b. how to make arms.

c. was Daniel.

B **Unscramble and write.**

1. a boy. | Mick | about | read

   →

2. used | to make arms | He | a 3-D printer | for Daniel.

   →

3. gave | He | his computer | the village | and 3-D printer.

   →

Technology

Word Review

A Choose and write.

| life | closer | bring | change | healthier | easier |

1.

_____

2.

_____

3.

_____

4.

_____

5.

_____

6.

_____

B Read and choose.

1. Technology has made our lives fun.

    ☐

2. Look at the timeline.

    ☐

 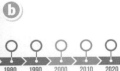

Sentence Review

A) Read and match.

1. How have technologies

2. Technology has made

3. It has helped bring

a) people closer together.

b) our lives healthier.

c) changed our lives?

B) Unscramble and write.

1. | has made | Technology | easier. | our lives |

   →

2. | has made | our lives | Technology | fun. |

   →

3. | some technologies | It | our lives. | that have changed | shows |

   →

UNIT 15

3-D Movies

Word Review

A Choose and write.

| burst | favorite | Friday | first | experience | lab |

1.

4 5 6 7
11 12 (13) 14
18 19 20

_____

2.

_____

3.

_____

4.

_____

5.

_____

6.

_____

B Read and choose.

1. It looked real on my 3-D glasses.

☐

2. Today was my family movie day.

☐

a   b

30

Sentence Review

A **Read and match.**

1. He looked

2. Every Friday, we go

3. He burst outside

a so happy.

b to a movie.

c to be free of his wheelchair.

B **Unscramble and write.**

1. we | the 3-D movie | Today, | watched | *Avatar.*

   →

2. He | from | the lab. | jumped up

   →

3. you | watch | hope | I | in 3-D. | *Avatar*

   →

UNIT 16

Social Media

Word Review

A Choose and write.

| learn | use | share | information | connected | topic |

1.

_____

2.

_____

3.

_____

4.

_____

5.

_____

6.

_____

B Read and choose.

1. You can share funny videos and photos. ☐

2. Moreover, most of it is free! ☐

Sentence Review

A **Read and match.**

1. Social media can

2. You can stay connected with

3. Enjoy

a friends and family members.

b your social media!

c be good for you.

B **Unscramble and write.**

1. | chat online | You | about | you like. | any topic | can |

→

2. | do better | You | can | in school. |

→

3. | social media | every day. | You | your | use | can |

→

Raise Money

Word Review

A Choose and write.

sell	expensive	buy	raise money	cheap	broken

1.
_____

2.
_____

3.
_____

4.
_____

5.
_____

6.
_____

B Read and choose.

1. We need to buy <u>wrapping papers</u>.

2. Let's think about the <u>price</u>.

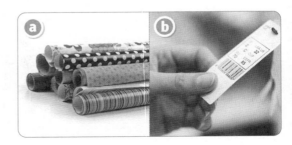

Sentence Review

A **Read and match.**

1.   Why don't we

2.   How about

3.   That's too

a   1,000 won for a toy?

b   expensive.

c   wash cars?

B **Unscramble and write.**

1.   are thinking   to raise money.   about   Leo and Sue   ways

→

2.   don't   old toys?   Why   sell   we

→

3.   our toys.   will   No one   buy

→

History of Money

Word Review

Ⓐ Choose and write.

| invent without swap payment invisible paper money |

1.
_____

2.
_____

3.
_____

4.
_____

5.
_____

6.
_____

Ⓑ Read and choose.

1. People started to use <u>coins</u> to buy things. ☐

2. The <u>credit card</u> was invented in the 1950s. ☐

Sentence Review

A **Read and match.**

1. People didn't need to

2. Instead of money,

3. People lived without

a. carry money any more.

b. money in 9000 B.C.

c. people swapped things.

B **Unscramble and write.**

1. | things | People | with shells. | bought |

→

2. | to buy | paper money | started to use | things. | People |

→

3. | most money | in the world | is | invisible. | Today, |

→

Matt's Pancakes

Word Review

A **Choose and write.**

| flour | combine | bowl | spread | top | mix |

1.

_____

2.

_____

3.

_____

4.

_____

5.

_____

6.

_____

B **Read and choose.**

1. He looks inside his mom's recipe book. ☐

2. He beats eggs in another bowl. ☐

Sentence Review

A **Read and match.**

1. He thinks of

2. Do you know how

3. He tops his pancake

a to make pancakes?

b some pancakes.

c with ice cream.

B **Unscramble and write.**

1. | made | He | pancakes | before. | has never |

   →

2. | He | the egg mixture | combines | and the flour mixture. |

   →

3. | is | ready! | Now, | the pancake |

   →

Kitchen Chemistry

Word Review

A Choose and write.

science drop stir liquid chemical reaction food coloring

1.
_____

2.
_____

3.
_____

4.
_____

5.
_____

6.
_____

B Read and choose.

1. Find a clean cotton swab. ☐

2. Pour some milk in a plate. ☐

Sentence Review

A **Read and match.**

1. What

2. It's important

3. A chemical reaction

a happens when matter changes.

b happened?

c not to stir the milk.

B **Unscramble and write.**

1. | a type of | Chemistry | is | science. |

→

2. | touch | Just | with | the cotton swab. | it |

→

3. | about | It | how | is | matter | changes. |

→

Unit 01. Scary Night

Word Review **B** **1.** ⓑ **2.** ⓐ

Sentence Review

A **1.** ⓑ **2.** ⓐ **3.** ⓒ

B **1.** We have a sleepover party at Ben's.
2. We fly like a witch.
3. We shake like a skeleton.

Unit 02. The Laser Maze

Word Review **B** **1.** ⓑ **2.** ⓐ

Sentence Review

A **1.** ⓐ **2.** ⓑ **3.** ⓒ

B **1.** Make a laser maze.
2. The fastest player wins the game.
3. Each player navigates through the laser maze.

Unit 03. My Best Birthday

Word Review **B** **1.** ⓐ **2.** ⓑ

Sentence Review

A **1.** ⓐ **2.** ⓒ **3.** ⓑ

B **1.** We cheered for the home team.
2. The batter stood at home plate.
3. It was my best birthday ever!

Unit 04. We Love and Care

Word Review **B** **1.** ⓑ **2.** ⓐ

Sentence Review

A **1.** ⓒ **2.** ⓑ **3.** ⓐ

B **1.** Family members have fun together.
2. Amy's mother teaches Amy to play the guitar.
3. Nate helps his father by feeding the dog.

Unit 05. The Treehouse

Word Review **B** **1.** ⓑ **2.** ⓐ

Sentence Review

A **1.** ⓑ **2.** ⓐ **3.** ⓒ

B **1.** Let's order some pizza!
2. I can do lots of cool things in it.
3. We put up the board for the roof.

Unit 06. Pizza for Kings and Queens

Word Review **B** **1.** ⓑ **2.** ⓐ

Sentence Review

A **1.** ⓒ **2.** ⓐ **3.** ⓑ

B **1.** The baker made a pizza of the Italian flag.
2. He used tomatoes for red.
3. The king and queen loved it.

Unit 07. We Are Friends

Word Review **B** **1.** ⓑ **2.** ⓐ

Sentence Review

A **1.** ⓒ **2.** ⓑ **3.** ⓐ

B **1.** We feel pleasure.
2. Just like us, animals have feelings.
3. It's not friendly to use animals for testing shampoo.

Unit 08. Save the Tigers

Word Review Ⓑ **1.** ⓐ **2.** ⓑ

Sentence Review

Ⓐ **1.** ⓑ **2.** ⓐ **3.** ⓒ

Ⓑ **1.** How much can a tiger weigh?
2. A jaguar can weigh up to 120 kg.
3. Many tigers have become extinct.

Unit 09. Fly's First Flight

Word Review Ⓑ **1.** ⓑ **2.** ⓐ

Sentence Review

Ⓐ **1.** ⓐ **2.** ⓑ **3.** ⓒ

Ⓑ **1.** Fly's father went into the air.
2. He almost touched the ceiling.
3. Fly flapped his wings up and down really fast.

Unit 10. A Horrible Swimmer

Word Review Ⓑ **1.** ⓐ **2.** ⓑ

Sentence Review

Ⓐ **1.** ⓑ **2.** ⓒ **3.** ⓐ

Ⓑ **1.** It prefers walking to swimming.
2. It has red lipstick-like lips.
3. It is a horrible swimmer.

Unit 11. Up

Word Review Ⓑ **1.** ⓐ **2.** ⓑ

Sentence Review

Ⓐ **1.** ⓐ **2.** ⓒ **3.** ⓑ

Ⓑ **1.** The hot-air balloon scraped the treetops.
2. There are no more bags of sand!
3. Soon, the hot-air balloon went up into the sky.

Unit 12. Energy

Word Review Ⓑ **1.** ⓐ **2.** ⓑ

Sentence Review

Ⓐ **1.** ⓑ **2.** ⓐ **3.** ⓒ

Ⓑ **1.** We use energy all the time.
2. We use electricity to charge cell phones.
3. We get energy from the sun, wind, and food.

Unit 13. Not Impossible

Word Review Ⓑ **1.** ⓐ **2.** ⓑ

Sentence Review

Ⓐ **1.** ⓒ **2.** ⓑ **3.** ⓐ

Ⓑ **1.** Mick read about a boy.
2. He used a 3-D printer to make arms for Daniel.
3. He gave the village his computer and 3-D printer.

Unit 14. Technology

Word Review Ⓑ **1.** ⓐ **2.** ⓑ

Sentence Review

Ⓐ **1.** ⓒ **2.** ⓑ **3.** ⓐ

Ⓑ **1.** Technology has made our lives easier.
2. Technology has made our lives fun.
3. It shows some technologies that have changed our lives.

Unit 15. 3-D Movies

Word Review Ⓑ 1. ⓑ 2. ⓐ
Sentence Review

Ⓐ 1. ⓐ 2. ⓑ 3. ⓒ

Ⓑ 1. Today, we watched the 3-D movie *Avatar*.
   2. He jumped up from the lab.
   3. I hope you watch *Avatar* in 3-D.

Unit 16. Social Media

Word Review Ⓑ 1. ⓑ 2. ⓐ
Sentence Review

Ⓐ 1. ⓒ 2. ⓐ 3. ⓑ

Ⓑ 1. You can chat online about any topic you like.
   2. You can do better in school.
   3. You can use your social media every day.

Unit 17. Raise Money

Word Review Ⓑ 1. ⓐ 2. ⓑ
Sentence Review

Ⓐ 1. ⓒ 2. ⓐ 3. ⓑ

Ⓑ 1. Leo and Sue are thinking about ways to raise money.
   2. Why don't we sell old toys?
   3. No one will buy our toys.

Unit 18. History of Money

Word Review Ⓑ 1. ⓑ 2. ⓐ
Sentence Review

Ⓐ 1. ⓐ 2. ⓒ 3. ⓑ

Ⓑ 1. People bought things with shells.
   2. People started to use paper money to buy things.
   3. Today, most money in the world is invisible.

Unit 19. Matt's Pancakes

Word Review Ⓑ 1. ⓑ 2. ⓐ
Sentence Review

Ⓐ 1. ⓑ 2. ⓐ 3. ⓒ

Ⓑ 1. He has never made pancakes before.
   2. He combines the egg mixture and the flour mixture.
   3. Now, the pancake is ready!

Unit 20. Kitchen Chemistry

Word Review Ⓑ 1. ⓑ 2. ⓐ
Sentence Review

Ⓐ 1. ⓑ 2. ⓒ 3. ⓐ

Ⓑ 1. Chemistry is a type of science.
   2. Just touch it with the cotton swab.
   3. It is about how matter changes.

미국교과서 리딩
READING

LEVEL 2 ③

Answer Key

Talk About It

- 당신은 친구 집에서 자본 적이 있나요?
- 그곳에서 무엇을 했나요?

Words to Know

듣고 따라 말해 보세요.

- costume 의상
- scary 무서운
- ghost 유령
- howl (길게) 울다
- scream 소리 지르다
- treat 간식
- witch 마녀
- skeleton 해골

Main Reading

우리는 벤의 집에서 밤샘 파티를 해요.
우리는 의상을 입고 정말 크게 소리를 질러요.
우리는 무서운 이야기들을 하고 많은 간식을 먹죠.
우리는 많은 게임을 하고 박자에 맞춰 춤을 춰요.
우리는 유령처럼 걸어다녀요.
우리는 마녀처럼 날아요.
우리는 늑대 인간처럼 울부짖어요.
우리는 해골처럼 흔들어요.
와, 정말 무서운 밤이에요!

Key Expressions

A: 너는 벤의 파티에서 무엇을 했니?
B: 나는 유령처럼 걸어다녔어.

| 문제 정답 및 해설 |

Comprehension Check

읽고 알맞은 답을 고르세요.

1. 어떤 종류의 파티인가요? [정답 : b]
   a. 생일 파티   **b.** 밤샘 파티

2. 우리는 벤의 파티에서 무엇을 입나요? [정답 : b]
   a. 우리는 잠옷을 입어요.
   b. 우리는 의상을 입어요.

3. 그림 속에서, 우리는 <u>무서워하지</u> 않아요. [정답 : b]
   a. 행복한   **b.** 무서워하는

Sentence Focus

읽고 알맞은 문장을 고르세요.

1. □ 우리는 댄스 파티를 해요.
   ■ 우리는 밤샘 파티를 해요.

2. ■ 나는 마녀처럼 날아요.
   □ 나는 해골처럼 흔들어요.

3. ■ 정말 무서운 밤이에요!
   □ 정말 즐거운 밤이에요!

Word Practice

그림을 보고 퍼즐을 완성하세요.

1. witch   **2.** costume   **3.** scary   **4.** ghost

Visualization : 추론하기

주어진 단어를 이용해서 표를 완성하세요.

- (첫째 줄 왼쪽부터) <u>wear</u> / <u>wear</u>
  (둘째 줄 왼쪽부터) <u>treats</u> / <u>treats</u>

텍스트 단서	이미 알고 있는 것
– 우리는 의상을 <u>입어요</u>.	– 우리는 할로윈에 의상을 <u>입어요</u>.
– 우리는 많은 <u>간식</u>을 먹어요.	– 우리는 할로윈에 많은 <u>간식</u>을 먹어요.

⇨ 추론: 오늘은 할로윈이에요!

Talk About It

• 당신은 어떤 게임을 알고 있나요?
• 당신은 늦은 밤에 할 만한 게임을 알고 있나요?

Words to Know

듣고 따라 말해 보세요.

• laser 레이저
• hallway 복도
• navigate 길을 찾다
• stopwatch 스톱워치
• maze 미로
• crepe paper 주름종이
• adjust 조절하다
• player 선수

Main Reading

〈레이저 미로를 만들어요〉
복도에 레이저 미로를 만들어요.
주름종이를 가느다랗게 잘라요.
한쪽 끝을 높이 붙이세요. 나머지 한 쪽 끝은 낮게 붙이세요.
가느다란 종이 조각들을 복도를 따라 쭉 붙이세요.
레이저 미로 사이로 길을 찾아가 보세요.
레이저 미로를 조절해 보세요.
〈게임 방법〉
스톱워치를 작동하는 것으로 게임이 시작돼요.
각 선수는 레이저 미로를 통과하는 길을 찾아요.
선수들은 미로 줄을 건드려서는 안돼요.
경주 시간을 재세요.
가장 빠른 선수가 게임에서 승리해요.

Key Expressions

A: 너는 레이저 미로 게임을 어떻게 하는지 아니?
B: 응. 각 선수는 레이저 미로를 통과하는 길을 찾아.

| 문제 정답 및 해설 |

Comprehension Check

읽고 알맞은 답을 고르세요.

1. 무엇에 관한 글인가요? [정답 : a]
   a. 레이저 미로에 관한 글이에요.
   b. 즐거운 밤에 관한 글이에요.

2. 레이저 미로를 만들기 위해서는 무엇이 필요한가요? [정답 : b]
   a. 레이저 **b.** 주름종이와 테이프

3. 레이저 미로를 통과해서 길을 찾는 것은 재미있어요. [정답 : a]
   a. 길을 찾다 **b.** 만지다

Sentence Focus

읽고 알맞은 문장을 고르세요.

1. ■ 주름종이를 높이 붙여요.
   □ 주름종이를 낮게 붙여요.

2. □ 미로를 건드리는 것으로 게임이 시작돼요.
   ■ 스톱워치를 작동하는 것으로 게임이 시작돼요.

3. ■ 가장 빠른 선수가 게임에서 이겨요.
   □ 가장 빠른 선수가 경주를 시작해요.

Word Practice

그림을 보고 퍼즐을 완성하세요.

1. maze 2. hallway 3. navigate 4. player

Visualization : 주제와 세부사항

주어진 단어를 이용해서 표를 완성하세요.

· (왼쪽부터) Adjust / stopwatch
· 레이저 미로
· 만드는 방법: 복도에 만드세요. / 주름종이를 잘라 붙이세요. /
  레이저 미로를 조절하세요.
· 게임 방법: 스톱워치를 작동시켜요. / 레이저 미로를 통과해 길을
  찾으세요. / 경주 시간을 재세요. / 가장 빠른 선수가 이깁니다.

Talk About It

- 당신은 아빠와 무엇을 하는 것을 좋아하나요?
- 당신은 야구 경기에 가본 적이 있나요?

Words to Know

듣고 따라 말해 보세요.

- baseball 야구
- score 점수
- home plate 본루
- strike 스트라이크
- enter 들어가다
- tie 동점
- pitch 투구, 공을 던짐
- swing 휘두르다

Main Reading

내 생일이었어요.
아빠는 나를 야구 경기에 데리고 가셨죠.
베어즈 팀이 경기장에 들어왔어요.
"베어즈 팀 힘내라!" 우리는 홈 팀을 응원했어요.
마지막 이닝의 후반전에, 점수는 동점이었어요.
베어즈 팀 타자가 본루에 서서 대기했죠.
첫 번째 투구는 속구였어요.
"원 스트라이크!"
다음 투구는 느렸어요.
타자가 세게 휘둘렀고, 탕!
펑!
공이 높이 높이 날아갔어요!
내 생애 최고의 생일이었어요!

Key Expressions

A: 너는 생일에 무엇을 했니?
B: 아빠가 나를 야구 경기에 데리고 가셨어.

| 문제 정답 및 해설 |

Comprehension Check

읽고 알맞은 답을 고르세요.

1. 내 생일에 나는 어디에 갔나요?   [정답 : a]
   a. 나는 야구 경기에 갔어요.
   b. 나는 농구 경기에 갔어요.

2. 무엇이 내 생일을 최고의 생일로 만들었나요?   [정답 : a]
   a. 베어즈 팀의 승리   b. 야구를 하는 것

3. 베어즈 팀은 홈 팀이에요.   [정답 : a]
   a. 홈   b. 두 번째의

Sentence Focus

읽고 알맞은 문장을 고르세요.

1. ■ 선수들이 경기장에 들어왔어요.
   □ 선수들이 경기장에서 응원했어요.

2. ■ 점수는 동점이었어요.
   □ 점수는 3대 2였어요.

3. ■ 엄마가 나를 야구 경기에 데리고 가셨어요.
   □ 나는 TV로 야구 경기를 봤어요.

Word Practice

그림을 보고 퍼즐을 완성하세요.

1. baseball   **2.** strike   **3.** swing   **4.** tie

```
b a s e b a l l
    t
    r
s w i n g
    k
t i e
```

Visualization : 배경

주어진 단어를 이용해서 표를 완성하세요.

- (순서대로) baseball / tie
- 어디서? – 야구 경기에서
- 무엇을? – 우리는 홈팀을 응원했어요.
  - 점수는 동점이었어요.
  - 타자가 세게 휘둘렀고 탕!
  - 내 생애 최고의 생일이었어요!

Talk About It

- 당신의 가족은 몇 명인가요?
- 당신은 가족과 함께 무엇을 하는 것을 좋아하나요?

Words to Know

듣고 따라 말해 보세요.

- mother 어머니
- member 구성원
- guitar 기타
- have fun 즐겁게 지내다
- father 아버지
- feed 먹이를 주다
- family 가족
- hide-and-seek 숨바꼭질

Main Reading

가족은 매우 다양할 수 있어요.
어떤 아이들은 오직 한 명의 부모님과 함께 살아요.
다른 아이들은 어머니, 아버지와 함께 살죠.
가족 구성원들은 서로를 도와요.
네이트는 개에게 먹이를 주는 것으로 아버지를 도와요.
에이미의 어머니는 에이미에게 기타 치는 법을 가르쳐 주시죠.
가족 구성원들은 함께 즐겁게 지내요.
존은 아버지와 함께 케이크를 구워요.
베라는 어머니와 함께 숨바꼭질을 하죠.
가족 구성원들은 서로를 사랑해요.

Key Expressions

A: 너는 어떻게 부모님을 도와드리니?
B: 개에게 먹이를 주는 것으로 아버지를 도와.

| 문제 정답 및 해설 |

Comprehension Check

읽고 알맞은 답을 고르세요.

1. 무엇에 관한 글인가요?   [정답 : a]
   a. 가족들에 관한 글이에요.
   b. 아이들에 관한 글이에요.

2. 어떤 가족들은 어떻게 다른가요?   [정답 : b]
   a. 어떤 아이들은 그들의 부모님과 즐겁게 지내요.
   b. 어떤 아이들은 오직 한 명의 부모님과 함께 살아요.

3. 가족들은 다양할 수 있지만, 그들은 모두 서로를 사랑해요. [정답 : b]
   a. 살다   **b.** 사랑하다

Sentence Focus

읽고 알맞은 문장을 고르세요.

1. ■ 가족 구성원들은 서로를 도와요.
   □ 가족 구성원들은 다양할 수 있어요.

2. ■ 그녀의 어머니는 그녀에게 기타 치는 법을 가르치셔요.
   □ 그녀의 어머니는 그녀에게 케이크 굽는 법을 가르치셔요.

3. ■ 그는 개에게 먹이를 주는 것으로 아버지를 도와요.
   □ 그는 기타를 치는 것으로 아버지를 도와요.

Word Practice

그림을 보고 퍼즐을 완성하세요.

1. mother   **2.** member   **3.** feed   **4.** father

Visualization : 비교와 대조

주어진 단어를 이용해서 표를 완성하세요.

- (순서대로) help / fun

다른 점	같은 점	다른 점
어떤 가정 – 한 명의 부모님 과 살아요.	가족 구성원들 – 서로 도와요. – 함께 즐겁게 지내요. – 서로 사랑해요.	또 다른 가정 – 어머니, 아버지와 살아요.

Talk About It

· 당신은 꿈에 그리는 집이 있나요?

· 당신이 꿈에 그리는 집에 대해 말해줄 수 있나요?

Words to Know

듣고 따라 말해 보세요.

· build 짓다
· wood 목재
· trunk 나무의 몸통
· board 널빤지

· treehouse 나무 위의 집
· nail 못을 박다
· climb 오르다
· order 주문하다

Main Reading

나는 뒷마당에 나무 위의 집을 지을 거예요.

나는 그 안에서 멋진 일을 많이 할 수 있지요.

나는 할아버지의 도움을 조금 받아서 나무 위의 집을 짓기 시작해요.

우리는 목재를 잘라요.

올라갈 수 있도록 나무 몸통에 목재를 못으로 박아요.

바닥으로 쓸 목재에 못질을 해요.

벽으로 쓸 목재에 못질을 해요.

지붕으로 쓸 판자를 얹어요.

"이제 무엇을 하고 싶니?" 할아버지가 물으셔요.

"피자 주문해요!" 내가 외쳐요.

나의 나무 위의 집에서 피자를 먹는 것은 멋진 일이에요.

Key Expressions

A: 이제 너는 무엇을 하고 싶니?

B: 우리 피자 주문하자!

| 문제 정답 및 해설 |

Comprehension Check

읽고 알맞은 답을 고르세요.

1. 나는 지금 무엇을 하고 있나요? 　　　　　[정답 : a]
　　a. 나무 위의 집을 짓고 있어요.
　　b. 할아버지를 돕고 있어요.

2. 나는 나무 위의 집에서 무엇을 하길 원하나요? 　[정답 : a]

　　a. 나는 나무 위의 집에서 피자를 먹고 싶어요.

　　b. 나는 나무 위의 집을 주문하고 싶어요.

3. 나의 나무 위의 집은 뒷마당에 있어요. 　　　[정답 : a]
　　a. 나무 위의 집　　　**b.** 자전거

Sentence Focus

읽고 알맞은 문장을 고르세요.

1. □ 나는 목재를 잘라요.
　　■ 나는 목재에 못을 박아요.

2. ■ 나는 지붕으로 쓸 판자를 얹어요.
　　□ 나는 벽으로 쓸 판자에 못을 박아요.

3. □ 할아버지는 내가 나무 위의 집에 올라가도록 도와주셔요.
　　■ 할아버지는 내가 나무 위의 집을 만들도록 도와주셔요.

Word Practice

그림을 보고 퍼즐을 완성하세요.

1. nail　**2.** climb　**3.** board　**4.** trunk

Visualization : 배경

주어진 단어를 이용해서 표를 완성하세요.

· (순서대로) build / order

어디에서?	무엇을?
– 뒷마당에서	⇨ 할아버지와 나는 나무 위의 집을 지어요.
– 나무 위의 집에서	⇨ 할아버지와 나는 피자를 주문해요.

50

Talk About It

- 당신은 피자를 좋아하나요?
- 당신이 가장 좋아하는 피자는 무엇인가요?

Words to Know

듣고 따라 말해 보세요.

- Italy 이탈리아
- visit 방문하다
- baker 제빵사
- basil 바질
- king 왕
- pizzeria 피자 가게
- Italian flag 이탈리아 국기
- everyone 모든 사람

Main Reading

마르게리따 피자는 이탈리아에서 왔어요.

마르게리따 왕비의 이름을 따라 지어졌어요.

국왕 움베르토 1세와 마르게리따 왕비는 1889년에 나폴리를 방문했어요.

왕과 왕비는 한 피자 가게에 갔어요.

그들은 특별한 피자를 요청했어요.

제빵사는 이탈리아 국기 모양의 피자를 만들었어요.

그는 초록색을 위해 바질 잎을 사용했어요.

그는 흰색을 위해 치즈를 사용했어요.

그는 빨간색을 위해 토마토를 사용했어요.

왕과 왕비는 그것을 몹시 마음에 들어 했어요.

오늘날, 마르게리따 피자는 왕과 왕비만을 위한 것이 아니에요.

모두를 위한 것입니다.

Key Expressions

A: 마르게리따 피자는 어디에서 왔니?

B: 이탈리아에서 왔어.

| 문제 정답 및 해설 |

Comprehension Check

읽고 알맞은 답을 고르세요.

1. 무엇에 관한 글인가요?   [정답 : a]

   a. 피자에 관한 글이에요.

   b. 피자의 여왕에 관한 글이에요.

2. 마르게리따 피자는 어디에서 왔나요?   [정답 : a]

   a. 이탈리아   **b.** 캐나다

3. 마르게리따 피자는 마르게리따 왕비의 이름을 따서 지어졌어요.

   a. 만들어지다   **b.** 이름 지어지다   [정답 : b]

Sentence Focus

읽고 알맞은 문장을 고르세요.

1. ☐ 마르게리따 왕이 피자 가게를 방문했어요.

   ■ 마르게리따 왕비가 피자 가게를 방문했어요.

2. ■ 오늘날, 마르게리따 피자는 모두를 위한 것이에요.

   ☐ 오늘날, 마르게리따 피자는 왕과 왕비만을 위한 것이에요.

3. ■ 제빵사는 초록색을 위해 바질 잎을 사용했어요.

   ☐ 제빵사는 초록색을 위해 토마토를 사용했어요.

Word Practice

그림을 보고 퍼즐을 완성하세요.

1. pizzeria   **2.** visit   **3.** baker   **4.** king

Visualization : 이야기 구성 요소

주어진 단어를 이용해서 표를 완성하세요.

- (왼쪽부터) baker / loved

누가?	무엇을?	왜?
– 나폴리의 제빵사	– 이탈리아 국기 모양의 피자를 만들었어요.	⇨ 왕과 왕비가 특별한 피자를 요청했어요.
– 사람들	– 그 피자에 마르게리따 이름을 붙였어요.	⇨ 왕비는 그 피자를 좋아했어요.

Talk About It

- 사진을 보세요. 그들은 어떤 점에서 서로 닮았나요?
- 그들은 어떤 점에서 서로 다른가요?

Words to Know

듣고 따라 말해 보세요.

- feeling 감정
- pain 고통
- testing 실험
- circus 서커스
- pleasure 기쁨
- friendly 친절한
- down (새의) 부드러운 털
- shark's fin 상어 지느러미

Main Reading

우리는 감정을 가지고 있어요.
우리는 기쁨을 느껴요.
우리는 고통을 느껴요.
우리와 똑같이, 동물도 감정을 가지고 있어요.
동물은 기쁨을 느껴요.
동물은 고통을 느껴요.
동물은 우리의 친구예요.
샴푸를 실험하기 위해 동물을 이용하는 것은 친절하지 않아요.
부드러운 털 베개를 위해 동물을 이용하는 것은 친절하지 않아요.
서커스에 동물을 이용하는 것은 친절하지 않아요.
상어 지느러미 수프를 위해 동물을 이용하는 것은 친절하지 않아요.

Key Expressions

A: 너와 동물들은 어떤 점에서 서로 비슷하니?
B: 우리는 감정을 가지고 있어.

| 문제 정답 및 해설 |

Comprehension Check

읽고 알맞은 답을 고르세요.

1. 무엇에 관한 글인가요?　　　　　　　　[정답 : b]
   a. 어떻게 친구를 사귀는지에 관한 글이에요.
   b. 동물이 어떻게 우리의 친구인지에 관한 글이에요.

2. 동물과 사람은 어떻게 서로 닮았나요?　　[정답 : a]
   a. 둘 다 감정을 가지고 있어요.
   b. 둘 다 샴푸를 사용해요.

3. 우리와 똑같이, 동물도 기쁨과 <u>고통</u>을 느껴요.　　[정답 : b]
   a. 친구　　　　　　b. 고통

Sentence Focus

읽고 알맞은 문장을 고르세요.

1. □ 사람은 감정을 가지고 있어요.
   ■ 동물은 감정을 가지고 있어요.

2. ■ 동물들은 우리의 친구예요.
   □ 과학자들은 우리의 친구예요.

3. ■ 서커스에서 동물을 이용하는 것은 친절하지 않아요.
   □ 부드러운 털 베개를 위해 동물을 이용하는 것은 친절하지 않아요.

Word Practice

그림을 보고 퍼즐을 완성하세요.

1. feeling　**2.** testing　**3.** pleasure　**4.** down

Visualization : 저자의 의도

주어진 단어를 이용해서 표를 완성하세요.

- (순서대로) <u>feelings</u> / <u>friendly</u>
- 사실 1: 우리는 감정을 가지고 있어요.
- 사실 2: 우리와 똑같이 동물도 <u>감정</u>을 가지고 있어요.
- ⇨ 저자의 의도: 상어 지느러미 수프나 샴푸 실험을 위해 동물을 이용하는 것은 <u>친절하지</u> 않아요. 동물은 권리가 있어요!

Talk About It

- 호랑이들은 어디에 있나요?
- 두 호랑이들은 서로 어떻게 비슷하고 다른가요?

Words to Know

듣고 따라 말해 보세요.

- biggest 가장 큰
- weigh 무게가 ~나가다
- power 힘
- bravery 용기
- tiger 호랑이
- symbol 상징
- hunt 사냥하다
- extinct 멸종된

Main Reading

〈가장 큰 고양잇과 동물〉

호랑이는 세계에서 가장 큰 고양잇과 동물입니다.
한 마리는 어느 정도 무게가 나갈 수 있을까요?
호랑이 한 마리는 300 킬로그램까지 무게가 나갈 수 있어요.
•호랑이 •사자 •재규어 •퓨마 •표범

〈큰 고양잇과 동물, 적은 개체 수〉

호랑이는 힘의 상징이에요.
하지만 어떤 사람들은 호랑이를 사냥하는 것을 용감함의 상징이라고
생각했어요. 많은 호랑이들이 지난 30년 사이에 멸종되었어요.
•호랑이의 개체 수

Key Expressions

A: 호랑이 한 마리는 무게가 어느 정도 나갈 수 있니?
B: 300 킬로그램까지 나갈 수 있어.

| 문제 정답 및 해설 |

Comprehension Check

읽고 알맞은 답을 고르세요.

1. 무엇에 관한 글인가요?　　　　　　　　　　[정답 : b]
　　a. 고양이에 관한 글이에요.
　　b. 호랑이에 관한 글이에요.

2. 호랑이는 무엇을 상징하나요?　　　　　　　[정답 : b]
　　a. 멸종　　　　　　**b.** 힘

3. 세계에서 가장 큰 고양잇과 동물은 <u>호랑이</u>입니다.　[정답 : a]
　　a. 호랑이　　　　　**b.** 표범

Sentence Focus

읽고 알맞은 문장을 고르세요.

1. ☐ 호랑이는 300 킬로그램까지 무게가 나갈 수 있어요.
　　■ 퓨마는 100 킬로그램까지 무게가 나갈 수 있어요.

2. ■ 호랑이를 사냥하는 것은 용감함의 상징이에요.
　　☐ 호랑이를 사냥하는 것은 사랑의 상징이에요.

3. ☐ 많은 호랑이들이 강해졌어요.
　　■ 많은 호랑이들이 멸종했어요.

Word Practice

그림을 보고 퍼즐을 완성하세요.

1. power　**2.** symbol　**3.** weigh　**4.** bravery

Visualization : 원인과 결과

주어진 단어를 이용해서 표를 완성하세요.

· (순서대로) <u>weigh</u> / <u>hunted</u> / <u>extinct</u>

왜인가요?	무슨 일이 일어났나요?
– 호랑이는 300 킬로그램까지 <u>무게가 나가요</u>.	⇨ 호랑이는 세계에서 가장 큰 고양잇과 동물이에요.
– 사람들이 호랑이를 <u>사냥해왔 어요</u>.	⇨ 많은 호랑이들이 <u>멸종</u>했어요.

Talk About It

- 새로운 무엇인가를 시도해본 적이 있나요?
- 처음 시도했을 때 느낌이 어땠나요?

Words to Know

듣고 따라 말해 보세요.

- flight 비행
- air 공중
- swing 그네를 타다
- flap (날개를) 퍼덕거리다
- doorknob (문의) 손잡이
- fly 날다
- ceiling 천장
- wing 날개

Main Reading

"비행하기에 좋은 날이구나!" 플라이의 아빠가 말했어요.
그래서 플라이와 아빠는 문손잡이로 갔어요.
플라이의 아빠가 공중으로 갔어요. 붕!
그런데 플라이는 어디에 있죠?
"플라이! 어서 오렴, 날아보자." 아빠가 말했어요.
"아뇨, 아뇨. 저는 나는 법을 몰라요.
저는 그네를 타고 싶어요." 플라이가 말했어요.
플라이는 높게 그네를 타서 거의 천장에 닿았어요.
그는 매우 높게 그네를 탔어요. 부웅!
그는 공중으로 날아갔어요.
"도와줘요!" 플라이가 외쳤어요.
"날개를 위아래로 퍼덕거리렴!" 그의 아빠가 소리쳤어요.
플라이는 날개를 위아래로 매우 빠르게 퍼덕거렸어요.
그리고 무슨 일이 벌어졌을까요?
"아빠, 저 날 수 있어요!" 플라이가 노래했어요.
이제, 플라이는 날 수 있답니다.

Key Expressions

A: 나는 나는 법을 몰라.   B: 날개를 위아래로 퍼덕거려 봐.

| 문제 정답 및 해설 |

Comprehension Check

읽고 알맞은 답을 고르세요.

1. 이야기 속의 등장인물들은 누구인가요?   [정답 : b]

a. 플라이와 그의 친구들   **b.** 플라이와 그의 아빠

2. 플라이에게 무슨 문제가 있나요?   [정답 : a]

a. 그는 나는 방법을 몰라요.

b. 그는 나는 것을 좋아하지 않아요.

3. 플라이는 <u>문손잡이</u>에서 그네를 타요.   [정답 : b]

a. 천장   **b.** 문손잡이

Sentence Focus

읽고 알맞은 문장을 고르세요.

1. □ 나는 문손잡이로 가고 싶어요.
   ■ 나는 그네를 타고 싶어요.

2. ■ 그는 거의 천장에 닿았어요.
   □ 그는 거의 그의 아빠에게 닿았어요.

3. ■ 그것은 날개를 위아래로 퍼덕거렸어요.
   □ 그것은 매우 높이 그네를 탔어요.

Word Practice

그림을 보고 퍼즐을 완성하세요.

1. flight   **2.** flap   **3.** wing   **4.** ceiling

Visualization : 다시 말해보기

주어진 단어를 이용해서 표를 완성하세요.

- (순서대로) <u>fly</u> / <u>air</u>
- 플라이는 <u>나는</u> 방법을 몰라서 그네를 탔어요.
- 플라이는 너무 높이 그네를 타서 <u>공중</u>으로 날아갔어요.
- 플라이는 날개를 아주 빠르게 퍼덕거렸어요.
  이제 그는 날 수 있어요!

Talk About It

- 당신은 수족관에 가본 적이 있나요?
- 당신은 물고기에 대해 무엇을 알고 있나요?

Words to Know

듣고 따라 말해 보세요.

- strange 이상한
- slight 작고 여윈, 갸날픈
- lips 입술
- prefer 선호하다
- broad 넓은
- lipstick 립스틱
- ocean floor 해저
- attack 공격하다

Main Reading

이 붉은입술부치는 이상하게 생겼어요.
넓적한 머리와 홀쭉한 몸을 가졌죠.
코처럼 생긴 긴 지느러미도 있어요.
빨간 립스틱을 바른 것 같은 입술이 있고요.
발처럼 생긴 지느러미도 있어요.
붉은입술부치는 해저에서 발견될 수 있어요.
그것은 해저를 걷기 위해 발처럼 생긴 지느러미를 사용해요.
헤엄치기보다 걷는 것을 더 좋아한답니다.
작은 물고기를 공격하기 위해 코 모양의 긴 지느러미를 사용해요.
길이는 40 센티미터까지 자라요.

- 코 모양의 긴 지느러미
- 빨간 립스틱을 바른 것 같은 입술
- 발처럼 생긴 지느러미
- 해저에서 쉬고 있는 붉은입술부치

Key Expressions

A: 붉은입술부치에 대해 무엇을 알고 있니?
B: 그것은 끔찍하게 수영을 못해.

| 문제 정답 및 해설 |

Comprehension Check

읽고 알맞은 답을 고르세요.

1. 무엇에 관한 글인가요? [정답 : b]

a. 수족관에 관한 글이에요.
b. 붉은입술부치에 관한 글이에요.

2. 붉은입술부치는 어떻게 이동하나요? [정답 : b]

a. 해저 위를 헤엄쳐요.
b. 해저를 걸어다녀요.

3. 붉은입술부치는 <u>발처럼 생긴 지느러미</u>로 이동해요. [정답 : b]

a. 립스틱을 바른 것 같은 입술
b. 발처럼 생긴 지느러미

Sentence Focus

읽고 알맞은 문장을 고르세요.

1. □ 이 붉은입술부치는 불가사리처럼 생겼어요.
   ■ 이 붉은입술부치는 이상하게 생겼어요.

2. ■ 그것은 빨간 립스틱을 바른 것 같은 입술을 가졌어요.
   □ 그것은 빨간 립스틱을 바른 것 같은 지느러미를 가졌어요.

3. ■ 그것은 헤엄치기보다 걷는 것을 더 좋아해요.
   □ 그것은 걷기보다 헤엄치는 것을 더 좋아해요.

Word Practice

그림을 보고 퍼즐을 완성하세요.

1. strange 2. slight 3. attack 4. prefer

Visualization : 설명과 도표

주어진 단어를 이용해서 표를 완성하세요.

- (순서대로) <u>lips</u> / <u>feet</u>
- 이것은 붉은입술부치의 사진이에요.
- 코 모양의 긴 지느러미: 작은 물고기를 공격해요.
- 빨간 립스틱을 바른 것 같은 <u>입술</u>: 이상해 보여요.
- <u>발</u>처럼 생긴 지느러미: 해저를 걸어요.

Talk About It

- 당신은 소풍 가는 것을 좋아하나요?
- 당신은 소풍 바구니 안에 무엇을 싸고 싶은가요?

Words to Know

듣고 따라 말해 보세요.

- hot-air balloon 열기구
- take off 이륙하다
- treetop 나무 꼭대기
- drop 떨어뜨리다
- basket 바구니
- scrape 긁다
- higher 더 높이
- steeple 첨탑

Main Reading

세 친구가 소풍 바구니를 들고 열기구 바구니에 탔어요.
"우리는 위로 올라갈 거야!" 그들이 외쳤어요.
열기구가 이륙했어요.
열기구가 나무 꼭대기를 긁었어요.
"우리 더 높이 올라갈 수 있을까?" 양이 물었어요.
당나귀는 모래 주머니 하나를 떨어뜨렸어요.
열기구가 지붕 꼭대기를 긁었어요.
"우리 더 높이 올라갈 수 있을까?" 돼지가 물었어요.
당나귀는 또 하나의 모래 주머니를 떨어뜨렸어요.
열기구가 첨탑을 긁었어요.
"우리 더 높이 올라갈 수 있을까?" 양이 물었죠.
"더이상은 모래 주머니가 없어!" 돼지가 외쳤어요.
곧 열기구는 하늘 높이 올라갔어요.
당나귀가 무슨 일을 했을까요?

Key Expressions

A: 우리 더 높이 올라갈 수 있니?   B: 물론이지.

| 문제 정답 및 해설 |

Comprehension Check

읽고 알맞은 답을 고르세요.

1. 무엇에 관한 이야기인가요?   [정답 : b]
   a. 열기구 경주에 관한 이야기예요.
   b. 열기구 타기에 관한 이야기예요.

2. 마지막에 열기구는 어떻게 하늘 높이 올라갔을까요?   [정답 : b]
   a. 당나귀가 모래 주머니를 떨어뜨렸어요.
   b. 당나귀가 소풍 바구니를 떨어뜨렸어요.

3. 세 친구는 당나귀, 돼지, 그리고 양이에요.   [정답 : b]
   a. 소   b. 돼지

Sentence Focus

읽고 알맞은 문장을 고르세요.

1. ■ 세 친구가 열기구 바구니에 탔어요.
   □ 세 친구가 소풍 바구니에 탔어요.

2. ■ 열기구가 나무 꼭대기를 긁었어요.
   □ 열기구가 지붕 꼭대기를 긁었어요.

3. □ 열기구가 도착했어요.   ■ 열기구가 이륙했어요.

Word Practice

그림을 보고 퍼즐을 완성하세요.

1. steeple   2. scrape   3. basket   4. take off

Visualization : 등장인물

주어진 단어를 이용해서 표를 완성하세요.

- (순서대로) higher / higher / dropped

등장인물	무엇을 했나요?
– 양	⇨ 당나귀에게 더 높이 올라갈 수 있는지 물었어요.
– 돼지	⇨ 당나귀에게 더 높이 올라갈 수 있는지 물었어요.
– 당나귀	⇨ 하늘 더 높이 올라가기 위해 소풍 바구니를 떨어뜨렸어요.

Talk About It

- 사람들은 에너지를 어떻게 사용하나요?
- 사람들은 어디에서 에너지를 얻나요?

Words to Know

듣고 따라 말해 보세요.

- talk 말하다
- resource 자원
- heat 따뜻하게 만들다
- cell phone 휴대폰
- think 생각하다
- electricity 전기
- charge 충전하다
- basketball 농구

Main Reading

우리는 항상 에너지를 사용해요.

우리는 걸을 때 에너지를 사용해요.

우리는 말할 때 에너지를 사용해요.

우리는 생각할 때 에너지를 사용해요.

우리는 심지어 잠을 잘 때도 에너지를 사용해요.

우리는 여러 자원으로부터 에너지를 얻어요.

우리는 태양, 바람, 전기, 그리고 음식으로부터 에너지를 얻어요.

우리는 건물을 따뜻하게 하기 위해서 태양 에너지를 사용할 수 있어요.

우리는 배로 항해하기 위해 바람을 사용할 수 있어요.

우리는 휴대폰을 충전하기 위해 전기를 사용해요.

우리가 음식으로부터 에너지를 얻으면, 우리는 농구를 할 수 있어요.

Key Expressions

A: 너는 에너지로 무엇을 할 수 있니?

B: 나는 생각하는 것에 에너지를 쓸 수 있어.

| 문제 정답 및 해설 |

Comprehension Check

읽고 알맞은 답을 고르세요.

1. 무엇에 관한 글인가요?   [정답 : a]

    a. 우리가 어떻게 에너지를 사용하는지에 관한 글이에요.

    b. 우리가 어떻게 휴대폰을 사용하는지에 관한 글이에요.

2. 우리는 언제 에너지를 사용하나요?   [정답 : a]

    a. 우리는 항상 에너지를 사용해요.

    b. 우리는 놀 때만 에너지를 사용해요.

3. 우리는 <u>태양</u>으로부터 에너지를 얻어요.   [정답 : b]

    a. 농구   **b.** 태양

읽고 알맞은 문장을 고르세요.

1. ☐ 우리는 말할 때 에너지를 사용해요.

    ■ 우리는 생각할 때 에너지를 사용해요.

2. ■ 우리는 음식으로부터 에너지를 얻어요.

    ☐ 우리는 전기로부터 에너지를 얻어요.

3. ☐ 우리는 연을 날리기 위해 바람을 이용해요.

    ■ 우리는 배로 항해하기 위해 바람을 이용해요.

Word Practice

그림을 보고 퍼즐을 완성하세요.

1. think   **2.** heat   **3.** charge   **4.** talk

Visualization : 원인과 결과

주어진 단어를 이용해서 표를 완성하세요.

· (왼쪽부터) <u>charge</u> / <u>talk</u>

왜인가요?	무슨 일이 일어났나요?
– 우리는 음식으로부터 에너지를 얻어요.	⇨ 우리는 걷고, <u>말하고</u>, 놀고, 생각할 수 있어요.
– 우리는 전기로 휴대폰을 <u>충전해요</u>.	⇨ 우리는 휴대폰을 사용할 수 있어요.

Talk About It

- 당신은 이 남자에 대해 어떻게 생각하나요?
- 이 사람을 돕는 것이 가능하다고 생각하나요? 왜 그렇게 생각하나요? 혹은 왜 그렇지 않다고 생각하나요?

Words to Know

듣고 따라 말해 보세요.

- arm 팔
- bombing 폭격
- 3-D printer 3D 프린터
- village 마을, 마을 사람들
- blow off (폭탄으로) 날려 버리다
- travel 여행하다
- teach 가르치다
- Sudanese 수단 사람

Main Reading

믹은 한 소년에 대한 글을 읽었어요.
그 소년의 이름은 다니엘이었어요.
다니엘은 수단에 살고 있었어요.
다니엘의 두 팔은 폭격 동안에 사라져 버렸어요.
믹은 다니엘에게 도움이 필요하다고 생각했죠.
그는 다니엘을 위해 무엇인가를 할 수 있다고 생각했어요.
믹은 수단으로 여행을 떠났어요.
그는 다니엘을 위한 두 팔을 만들기 위해 3D 프린터를 사용했어요.
그는 그 마을 사람들에게 팔을 만드는 방법을 가르쳐 줬어요.
그는 그의 컴퓨터와 3D 프린터를 마을에 줬어요.
이제 그 마을 사람들은 다른 수단 사람들을 도울 수 있어요.
마을 사람들이 그들을 위해 두 팔을 만들어 줄 수 있답니다.

Key Expressions

A: 너는 어떻게 다니엘을 도울 수 있니?
B: 나는 다니엘을 위한 두 팔을 만들기 위해 3D 프린터를 사용할 수 있어.

| 문제 정답 및 해설 |

Comprehension Check

읽고 알맞은 답을 고르세요.

1. 무엇에 관한 이야기인가요? [정답 : a]
   a. 다니엘에 관한 이야기예요.
   b. 수단에 대한 이야기예요.

2. 믹은 어떻게 다니엘을 도왔나요? [정답 : b]
   a. 믹은 다니엘에게 그의 3D 프린트를 줬어요.
   b. 믹은 다니엘을 위해 두 팔을 만들었어요.

3. 믹은 그 마을 사람들이 다른 수단 사람들을 돕도록 <u>가르쳤어요.</u>
   a. 줬다   b. 가르쳤다   [정답 : b]

Sentence Focus

읽고 알맞은 문장을 고르세요.

1. ■ 그는 한 소년에 대한 글을 읽었어요.
   □ 그는 한 소년에 대해 이야기 했어요.

2. ■ 그녀는 수단으로 여행을 떠났어요.
   □ 그녀는 수단에 살았어요.

3. ■ 그는 두 팔을 만들기 위해 3D 프린터를 사용했어요.
   □ 그는 수단에 가기 위해 3D 프린터를 사용했어요.

Word Practice

그림을 보고 퍼즐을 완성하세요.

1. travel   2. village   3. arm   4. teach

Visualization : 결론 내리기

주어진 단어를 이용해서 표를 완성하세요.

- (순서대로) bombing / Sudanese
- 사실 1: 다니엘의 두 팔은 <u>폭격</u> 동안 사라져 버렸어요.
- 사실 2: 믹은 다니엘을 위한 두 팔을 만들기 위해 3D 프린터를 사용했어요.
- ⇨ 결론: 다니엘 같은 다른 <u>수단 사람들</u>도 새 팔을 가질 수 있어요. 그것은 불가능하지 않아요!

Talk About It

- 기술이란 무엇일까요?
- 당신은 매일 어떤 기술들을 사용하고 있나요?

Words to Know

듣고 따라 말해 보세요.

- technology 기술
- easier 더 쉬운
- bring 가져오다
- timeline 연대표
- life 삶
- healthier 더 건강한
- closer 더 가까운
- change 바꾸다

Main Reading

기술은 우리의 삶을 더 쉽게 만들었어요.

기술은 우리의 삶을 더 건강하게 만들었어요.

기술은 우리의 삶을 재미있게 만들었어요.

또 사람들이 더 가깝게 모이도록 도와줬어요.

이 연대표를 보세요.

우리의 삶을 바꾼 기술들을 보여주고 있어요.

1973년: 휴대폰   1976년: 개인용 컴퓨터

1993년: 인터넷 서핑을 위한 웹 브라우저

2003년: 하이브리드 자동차   2007년: 아이폰 (스마트폰)

2009년: 전자 눈   2010년: 자율 주행 자동차

2014년: 3D 프린터   2022년: 챗GPT

Key Expressions

A: 기술이 우리 삶을 어떻게 바꾸었니?

B: 우리 삶을 재미있게 만들었어.

| 문제 정답 및 해설 |

Comprehension Check

읽고 알맞은 답을 고르세요.

1. 무엇에 관한 글인가요?   [정답 : b]

   a. 기술이 무엇인지에 관한 글이에요.

   b. 기술이 우리의 삶을 어떻게 바꿨는지에 관한 글이에요.

2. 3D 프린터는 언제 나왔나요?   [정답 : b]

   a. 2009년   **b.** 2014년

3. 챗GPT는 휴대폰 <u>이후에</u> 나왔습니다.   [정답 : b]

   a. 이전에   **b.** 이후에

Sentence Focus

읽고 알맞은 문장을 고르세요.

1. ☐ 기술은 우리 삶을 지루하게 만들었어요.

   ■ 기술은 우리 삶을 재미있게 만들었어요.

2. ■ 기술은 우리 삶을 더 건강하게 만들었어요.

   ☐ 기술은 우리 삶을 바꾸지 않았어요.

3. ■ 이것들은 몇 가지 기술들을 보여줘요.

   ☐ 이것들은 몇 가지 연대표들을 보여줘요.

Word Practice

그림을 보고 퍼즐을 완성하세요.

1. life   **2.** healthier   **3.** bring   **4.** technology

Visualization : 주제와 세부사항

주어진 단어를 이용해서 표를 완성하세요.

- (순서대로) <u>Technology</u> / <u>closer</u>
- 주제 – 기술
- 세부사항 – 그것은 삶을 더 쉽게 만들었어요.
  - 그것은 삶을 더 건강하게 만들었어요.
  - 그것은 삶을 재미있게 만들었어요.
  - 그것은 사람들이 더 <u>가깝게</u> 모이도록 도왔어요.

Talk About It

- 당신은 영화를 좋아하나요?
- 당신이 가장 좋아하는 영화는 무엇인가요?

Words to Know

듣고 따라 말해 보세요.

- movie 영화
- favorite 가장 좋아하는
- experience 경험
- burst 불쑥 나오다
- Friday 금요일
- first 첫 번째의
- lab 실험실
- 3-D glasses 3D 안경

Main Reading

다인에게,

오늘은 우리 가족 영화 감상의 날이었어.

매주 금요일마다 우리는 영화를 보러 가.

오늘 우리는 3D 영화인 〈아바타〉를 관람했어.

내가 가장 좋아하는 부분은 제이크가 처음으로 그의 아바타 몸을 경험하는 부분이었어.

그는 정말 행복해 보였지.

그는 실험실에서 뛰어올랐어.

그는 휠체어에서 벗어나 밖으로 불쑥 나왔지.

3D 안경으로 보니 정말 진짜처럼 보였어.

제이크의 아바타가 내 앞에서 달리고 있는 것처럼 느껴졌어.

너도 〈아바타〉를 3D로 보길 바래.

사랑을 담아서, 수가

Key Expressions

A: 너는 어제 무엇을 했니?

B: 우리 가족 영화 감상의 날이었어.

| 문제 정답 및 해설 |

Comprehension Check

읽고 알맞은 답을 고르세요.

1. 나는 무엇을 하고 있나요?   [정답 : b]
   a. 나는 다인과 이야기하고 있어요.
   b. 나는 이메일을 쓰고 있어요.

2. 우리 가족은 언제 영화를 보러 가나요?   [정답 : a]
   a. 매주 금요일   **b.** 매일

3. 진짜처럼 보이기 때문에 나는 3D 영화 보는 것을 좋아해요.
   a. 안경   **b.** 영화   [정답 : b]

Sentence Focus

읽고 알맞은 문장을 고르세요.

1. ■ 매주 금요일마다 우리는 영화를 보러 가요.
   □ 매주 금요일마다 우리는 실험실에 가요.

2. ■ 이것이 그 영화에서 내가 가장 좋아하는 부분이에요.
   □ 이것이 그 책에서 내가 가장 좋아하는 부분이에요.

3. ■ 3D 안경으로 보니 정말 진짜처럼 보여요.
   □ 3D 안경으로 보니 정말 슬퍼 보여요.

Word Practice

그림을 보고 퍼즐을 완성하세요.

1. favorite   **2.** Friday   **3.** movie   **4.** burst

Visualization : 배경

주어진 단어를 이용해서 표를 완성하세요.

- (순서대로) Friday / 3-D glasses

언제?	무엇을?
– 금요일	– 우리는 3D 영화를 봤어요.
어디서?	– 우리는 3D 안경을 썼어요.
– 극장에서	– 정말 진짜처럼 보였어요.

Talk About It

- 당신은 스마트폰을 가지고 있나요?
- 당신은 언제 스마트폰을 사용하나요?

Words to Know

듣고 따라 말해 보세요.

- learn 배우다
- share 공유하다
- use 사용하다
- information 정보
- connected 연결된
- funny 재미있는
- topic 주제
- free 무료의

Main Reading

당신은 소셜 미디어를 매일 사용할 수 있어요.
당신은 친구, 가족과 연결된 상태를 유지할 수 있어요.
당신은 재미있는 영상과 사진을 공유할 수 있어요.
당신은 좋아하는 어떤 주제에 대해서 온라인으로 이야기를 나눌 수 있어요.
당신은 다른 사람들과 정보를 공유하고 그들로부터 배울 수 있어요.
그래서 당신은 학교에서 더 잘 해낼 수 있어요.
게다가, 대부분의 소셜 미디어는 무료예요!
소셜 미디어는 당신에게 좋은 영향을 줄 수 있어요.
소셜 미디어를 즐기세요!

Key Expressions

A: 너는 소셜 미디어로 무엇을 하니?
B: 나는 재미있는 영상을 공유해.

| 문제 정답 및 해설 |

Comprehension Check

읽고 알맞은 답을 고르세요.

1. 무엇에 관한 글인가요? [정답 : b]
   a. 소셜 미디어를 만드는 방법에 관한 글이에요.
   b. 소셜 미디어로 무엇을 할 수 있는지에 관한 글이에요.

2. 소셜 미디어로 무엇을 할 수 있나요? [정답 : a]
   a. 친구들과 사진을 공유할 수 있어요.
   b. 친구들과 장난감을 공유할 수 있어요.

3. 대부분의 소셜 미디어는 <u>무료</u>예요. [정답 : b]
   a. 더 나은   b. 무료의

Sentence Focus

읽고 알맞은 문장을 고르세요.

1. ■ 당신은 소셜 미디어를 매일 사용할 수 있어요.
   □ 당신은 소셜 미디어를 매일 구입할 수 있어요.

2. □ 나는 나의 주제를 공유할 수 있어요.
   ■ 나는 나의 영상을 공유할 수 있어요.

3. ■ 당신은 학교에서 더 잘 해낼 수 있어요.
   □ 당신은 소셜 미디어에서 더 잘 해낼 수 있어요.

Word Practice

그림을 보고 퍼즐을 완성하세요.

1. use   **2.** share   **3.** free   **4.** funny

Visualization : 원인과 결과

주어진 단어를 이용해서 표를 완성하세요.

· (순서대로) connected / learn

왜인가요?	무슨 일이 일어났나요?
– 소셜 미디어는 당신에게 좋은 영향을 줄 수 있어요.	⇨ 당신은 다른 사람들과 <u>연결된</u> 상태를 유지해요.
– 소셜 미디어는 학교에서 더 잘 해낼 수 있게 도와줘요.	⇨ 당신은 어떤 주제에 대해 소셜 미디어에서 <u>배워요</u>.

Talk About It

- 당신은 용돈을 마련해 본 적이 있나요?
- 용돈을 마련하기 위한 방법을 알고 있나요?

Words to Know

듣고 따라 말해 보세요.

- raise money (용)돈을 마련하다
- wrapping papers 포장지
- cheap (값이) 싼
- buy 사다
- broken 부러진
- sell 팔다
- expensive (값이) 비싼
- price 값

Main Reading

레오와 수는 용돈을 마련하는 방법을 생각해요.

"세차하는 것은 어때?"

"좋은 생각이야. 그런데 너는 다리를 다쳤잖아!"

"오래된 장난감을 판매하는 것은 어때?"

"멋진데!"

"장난감 하나에 1,000원은 어떨까?"

"너무 저렴해. 우리는 포장지와 리본을 구입해야 해. 그것만해도 1,000원일 거야."

"장난감 하나에 5,000원은 어때?"

"너무 비싸. 아무도 우리 장난감을 사지 않을 거야."

"맞아! 값을 신중하게 생각해보자."

"그래!"

Key Expressions

A: 너는 어떻게 용돈을 마련할 수 있니?
B: 나는 오래된 장난감을 판매할 수 있어.

| 문제 정답 및 해설 |

Comprehension Check

읽고 알맞은 답을 고르세요.

1. 누가 용돈을 마련하는 방법을 생각하고 있나요?   [정답 : b]
   a. 레오와 그의 엄마
   b. 레오와 수

2. 레오와 수는 용돈을 마련하기 위해 무엇을 하나요?   [정답 : b]
   a. 그들은 세차를 해요.
   b. 그들은 오래된 장난감을 팔아요.

3. 레오와 수는 값에 대해 신중하게 생각할 필요가 있어요.
   a. 값   b. 자동차   [정답 : a]

Sentence Focus

읽고 알맞은 문장을 고르세요.

1. □ 그것은 1,000원이에요.
   ■ 그것은 5,000원이에요.

2. ■ 우리는 포장지를 구입해야 해요.
   □ 우리는 리본을 구입해야 해요.

3. □ 장난감 하나에 1,000원은 어떤가요?
   ■ 장난감 하나에 2,000원은 어떤가요?

Word Practice

그림을 보고 퍼즐을 완성하세요.

1. cheap   2. sell   3. price   4. broken

Visualization : 주제와 세부사항

주어진 단어를 이용해서 표를 완성하세요.

- (왼쪽부터) sell / expensive
- 주제 – 용돈을 마련해요.
- 세부사항 – 아이들은 세차를 할 수 있어요.
  아이들은 오래된 장난감을 판매할 수 있어요.
  – 값은 너무 저렴하지 않아야 해요.
  값은 너무 비싸지 않아야 해요.

Talk About It

- 이 가족은 어디에 있나요?
- 그들은 무엇을 하고 있나요?

Words to Know

듣고 따라 말해 보세요.

- swap 교환하다
- paper money 지폐
- credit card 신용카드
- payment 지불
- without ~ 없이
- coin 동전
- invent 발명하다
- invisible 보이지 않는

Main Reading

〈물물교환〉

기원전 9000년에 사람들은 화폐 없이 살았어요.
화폐 대신에, 사람들은 물물교환을 했어요.

〈최초의 화폐〉

3000년 전에, 사람들은 조개껍데기를 화폐로 사용했어요.
물물교환 대신에, 사람들은 조개껍데기로 물건을 구입했어요.

〈화폐〉

사람들은 물건을 사기 위해 지폐와 동전을 사용하기 시작했어요.

〈신용카드〉

신용카드는 1950년대에 발명되었어요. 사람들은 더이상 돈을 들고 다닐 필요가 없었어요.

〈온라인 결제〉

오늘날, 세상에 있는 대부분의 화폐는 눈에 보이지 않아요.

Key Expressions

A: 너는 아이패드를 어떻게 결제했니?
B: 온라인으로 결제했어.

| 문제 정답 및 해설 |

Comprehension Check

읽고 알맞은 답을 고르세요.

1. 무엇에 관한 글인가요?   [정답 : a]

   a. 화폐의 역사에 관한 글이에요.

   b. 기술의 역사에 관한 글이에요.

2. 요즘에는 대부분의 사람들이 어떻게 결제하나요?   [정답 : b]

   a. 물물교환으로   **b.** 온라인 결제로

3. 조개껍데기는 최초의 화폐로 사용되었어요.   [정답 : b]

   a. 신용카드   **b.** 조개껍데기

Sentence Focus

읽고 알맞은 문장을 고르세요.

1. ■ 사람들은 화폐 대신에 물물교환을 했어요.

   □ 사람들은 조개껍데기를 화폐로 사용했어요.

2. ■ 신용카드는 1950년대에 발명되었어요.

   □ 온라인 결제는 1950년대에 만들어졌어요.

3. ■ 오늘날, 세상에 있는 대부분의 화폐는 눈에 보이지 않아요.

   □ 오늘날, 세상에 있는 대부분의 화폐는 무거워요.

Word Practice

그림을 보고 퍼즐을 완성하세요.

1. coin   **2.** invent   **3.** invisible   **4.** swap

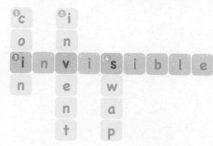

Visualization : 순서

주어진 단어를 이용해서 표를 완성하세요.

- (순서대로) shells / carry
- 기원전 9000년: 화폐가 없던 시절
- 기원전 1200년: 화폐로 조개껍데기를 사용했어요.
- 기원후 806년: 동전과 지폐
- 1950년대: 돈을 들고 다닐 필요가 없어요.
- 현재: 눈에 보이지 않는 돈

Talk About It

- 당신은 배가 고픈가요?
- 무엇을 먹고 싶은가요?

Words to Know

듣고 따라 말해 보세요.

- recipe 조리법
- flour 밀가루
- beat 휘저어 섞다
- spread 바르다
- mix 섞다
- bowl 그릇
- combine 결합시키다
- top 위에 올리다

Main Reading

맷은 배가 고파요.

그는 약간의 팬케이크가 생각나요.

그는 전에 팬케이크를 만들어 본 적이 없어요.

그는 엄마의 커다란 요리책을 들여다봐요.

그는 밀가루와 베이킹파우더를 그릇 안에 섞어요.

다음으로, 다른 그릇에 달걀을 깨서 휘저어요.

그런 다음에, 설탕과 우유를 넣어요.

마지막으로, 달걀 혼합물과 밀가루 혼합물을 합쳐요.

그는 혼합물을 프라이팬에 잘 펴놓고 3분 동안 구워요.

이제 팬케이크가 준비되었어요!

그는 팬케이크 위에 아이스크림을 올려요.

꿀꺽, 냠냠!

맷은 그의 첫 번째 팬케이크가 무척 마음에 들어요!

Key Expressions

A: 너는 팬케이크 만드는 방법을 아니?

B: 응.

| 문제 정답 및 해설 |

Comprehension Check

읽고 알맞은 답을 고르세요.

1. 무엇에 관한 글인가요?　　　　　　　　　[정답 : a]

　a. 팬케이크를 만드는 방법에 관한 글이에요.

　b. 맷이 팬케이크를 왜 좋아하는지에 관한 글이에요.

2. 맷은 왜 엄마의 요리책을 보나요?　　　　　[정답 : a]

　a. 그는 이전에 팬케이크를 만들어 본 적이 없기 때문이에요.

　b. 그는 엄마의 팬케이크 요리법을 좋아하기 때문이에요.

3. 맷은 그의 첫 번째 팬케이크가 무척 마음에 들어요.　[정답 : a]

　a. 첫 번째의　　　　**b.** 마지막의

Sentence Focus

읽고 알맞은 문장을 고르세요.

1.　■ 그는 그릇 안에 달걀을 깨서 휘저어요.

　　□ 그는 프라이팬 안에 달걀을 깨서 휘저어요.

2.　■ 그는 빵에 잼을 발라요.

　　□ 그는 혼합물을 프라이팬에서 구워요.

3.　□ 그는 팬케이크 위에 코코아를 올려요.

　　■ 그는 팬케이크 위에 아이스크림을 올려요.

Word Practice

그림을 보고 퍼즐을 완성하세요.

1. flour　**2.** bowl　**3.** recipe　**4.** combine

Visualization : 다시 말해보기

주어진 단어를 이용해서 표를 완성하세요.

- (순서대로) recipe / tops
- 왜? – 맷은 배가 고파요.
- 무엇을? – 맷은 엄마의 요리책을 들여다봐요.

　　　　그는 팬케이크를 구워요.

　　　　그는 그의 팬케이크 위에 아이스크림을 올려요.

Talk About It

· 남자아이는 무엇을 하고 있나요?
· 물질의 세 가지 상태는 무엇인가요?

Words to Know

듣고 따라 말해 보세요.

· science 과학
· plate 접시
· food coloring 식용 색소
· liquid 액체의
· chemical reaction 화학 반응
· drop 방울
· cotton swab 면봉
· stir 휘젓다

Main Reading

화학은 과학의 한 종류예요.
물질이 어떻게 변화하는지에 관한 것이죠.
물질이 변화할 때 화학 반응이 일어나요.
접시에 우유를 약간 따르세요.
서로 다른 네 가지 색의 식용 색소를 한 방울씩 더하세요.
깨끗한 면봉을 찾으세요.
액체 세제 한 방울을 면봉에 묻히세요.
우유를 휘젓지 않는 것이 중요해요.
면봉으로 살짝 건드리기만 하세요.
무슨 일이 일어났나요?
아름다운 그림이 우유의 표면 위에 나타납니다.
이것이 화학이랍니다.

· 화학반응

Key Expressions

A: 화학이 무엇이니?
B: 물질이 어떻게 변화하는지에 관한 거야.

| 문제 정답 및 해설 |

Comprehension Check

읽고 알맞은 답을 고르세요.

1. 무엇에 관한 글인가요? [정답 : b]
　a. 욕실 속 화학에 관한 글이에요.
　b. 주방 속 화학에 관한 글이에요.

2. 화학이 무엇인가요? [정답 : b]
　a. 물질이 무엇인가에 관한 것이에요.
　b. 물질이 어떻게 변화하는지에 관한 것이에요.

3. 그림에서, 거품들이 바로 화학 반응이에요. [정답 : a]
　a. 거품들　　　　**b.** 접시들

Sentence Focus

읽고 알맞은 문장을 고르세요.

1. □ 화학은 예술의 한 종류예요.
　■ 화학은 과학의 한 종류예요.

2. ■ 식용 색소 한 방울을 더하세요.
　□ 식용 색소 한 컵을 부으세요.

3. □ 우유를 휘젓는 것이 중요해요.
　■ 우유를 휘젓지 않는 것이 중요해요.

Word Practice

그림을 보고 퍼즐을 완성하세요.

1. drop　**2.** plate　**3.** stir　**4.** science

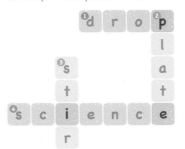

Visualization : 원인과 결과

주어진 단어를 이용해서 표를 완성하세요.

· (순서대로) reaction / liquid

원인	결과
– 물질이 변화해요.	⇨ 화학 반응이 일어나요.
– 우유, 식용 색소, 액체 세제를 섞었어요.	⇨ 아름다운 그림이 나타났어요.

미국교과서 READING Level 2 권별 교과 목록

1권 2.1

1. Social Studies
2. Language Arts
3. Health & Wellness
4. Language Arts
5. Health & Wellness
6. Social Studies
7. Social Studies
8. Health & Wellness
9. Social Studies
10. Science
11. Science
12. Math
13. Social Studies
14. Science
15. Social Studies
16. Math
17. Science
18. Science
19. Ethics
20. Science

2권 2.2

1. Health & Wellness
2. Science
3. Language Arts
4. Social Studies
5. Language Arts
6. Health & Wellness
7. Language Arts
8. Social Studies
9. Language Arts
10. Science
11. Language Arts
12. Language Arts
13. Ethics
14. Ethics
15. Language Arts
16. Science
17. Language Arts
18. Art & Crafts
19. Language Arts
20. Ethics

3권 2.3

1. Social Studies
2. Art & Crafts
3. Health & Wellness
4. Social Studies
5. Language Arts
6. Social Studies
7. Ethics
8. Social Studies
9. Language Arts
10. Science
11. Language Arts
12. Science
13. Social Studies
14. Science
15. Science
16. Science
17. Social Studies
18. Social Studies
19. Language Arts
20. Science